Learn Nahu

Language of the Aztecs and Modern Nahuas

Version 2

Yan Garcia
1tecuexe@gmail.com

Tlaskamatilistli

Nikintlaskamatilia nochi masewalmeh tlen nawatih, iwan nochimeh tlen nechmachtihketh inin yehyehtsin tlahtolli. Nikinstlaskamatilia nochi tlamachtianih tlen nechmachtihkeh: Victoriano, Eduardo, Abelardo, Catalina, Delfina, Ofelia, Delia, Sabina, Manuel iwan John. Nohkiya niktlaskamatilia ne ixtlamatihketl Magnus Pharao Hansen.

Nikintlaskamatilia nowampoyowan: Julio, Alex, Marco, Abel, Lucero, iwan tlamachtianih tlen Tlahtoltapasolli: Axolotl, Steph, Xika Ilwikasiwatl, Ekatlahtoa, Kenwel Tehwantin, Kwitlawak, Kolotl, Ricardo, Jesse, Rebecca, iwan Esai.

Nikintlaskamatilia notekixpoyowan tlen Nechikolli Se Ome Tlahtolli. Inkimanawiah totlahtol.

Ma yoli tonawatlahtol, ma momachtikan tokonetsitsin, ma nawatikan.

Contents

Introduction

The term Aztec refers to a large group of people who at one point in time migrated from Aztlan, a region whose location is still a mystery. There were several tribes that are believed to have migrated from Aztlan and they developed their own cities and competed for power. The Aztecs are also commonly known as the Mexicah, or people from the region of Mexico. They weren't the only ones to speak Nahuatl, however. The Acolhuas, the Tlaxcaltec, the Xochimilca, the Caxcan and even more groups spoke Nahuatl.

Today, the Nahuatl language is still very much alive and spoken by over a million people in Mexico, and a very closely related language Nawat/Pipil is still spoken in El Salvador, although it is highly endangered. Nahuatl is not spoken solely in one region, rather, it's spoken throughout dozens of regions and mostly in towns far removed from cities and urban centers. The unfortunate trend of moving towards Spanish has been going on for well over 300 years, and the pattern is usually the same; the larger the town, the faster it moves to Spanish.

There is a diaspora of people now in the United States whose ancestors spoke Nahuatl. For some people, this means their parents, for others, this means their great-grandparents, and still for others, the transition may have happened in the 1700s. We can only dream of how many millions of people would still be speaking Nahuatl today were it not for colonization. Perhaps Mexico may have developed like Japan, independent yet strongly rooted in its heritage.

The future of Nahuatl rests on the number of people who speak and/or value it. For this reason, I've decided to write this manual in English, for the Chicano people who wish to learn to speak Nahuatl as their heritage language, and for outsiders who value this language, since outside support is much required. Native speakers are usually intrigued when outsiders learn their language and it shows them that their language is indeed valuable. It is also important to mention that Mexico is home to over 64 languages, and many people may find their ancestral language to be one of these. I encourage the reader to research their heritage, but still consider that Nahuatl was the Lingua Franca (or main trade language) of ancient Mexico at one time.

I have written this book taking into consideration that not everyone is a linguist. Many language books published are written towards scholars, and are not very useful resources for the community. Consider this a guide written with the community in mind.

That being said, this book is not extensive enough to cover all major components of Nahuatl. Still, this guide should give you enough tools for you to self-learn.

The region with the most number of Nahuatl speakers is in the Huasteca, a region that is made up of parts of Hidalgo, Veracruz and San Luis Potosi. This guide is based on Huasteca Nahuatl, particularly the one spoken in the Chicontepec, Veracruz area. There are different varieties of Nahuatl just like there are different dialects of English (British English, Australian English, American English etc.). At times I'll include information on different varieties to help the reader become more familiar with the variation within Nahuatl.

Why Learn Nahuatl?

Nahuatl is the largest native American (indigenous to the Americas) language spoken in North America (over one and a half million). No native language in the U.S. comes close for second. Inside the borders of the U.S., Navajo is the largest indigenous language with over 100,000 speakers. But this is still about 1/10 of Nahuatl. The Mayan language Quiche comes close with about a million speakers, but in South America, Quechua, Aymara and Guarani have more speakers than Nahuatl.

Nahuatl was the language used by Aztecs, the Mexicah, Acolhua, Tlaxcaltecah and many more. During the colonial period, there were also documents written in Nahuatl from western Mexico like Jalisco, Colima and Zacatecas. Nahuatl speakers were also used by the Spanish to settle new regions as far away as New Mexico.

What's New?

This new, updated version of *Learn Nahuatl* contains much new information lacking in previous versions. For one, a much improved dictionary is attached to the end, and though not enough to contain all the vocabulary, is still a major improvement. Secondly, new exercises are included that focus on expansion of vocabulary and morphology (how words are broken into pieces). The biggest change is the adoption of the revised modern orthography promoted by INALI (Instituto Nacional de Lenguas Indígenas) as well as dozens of native speakers, leaders of their communities, who have gathered to unify their writing.

Uto-Aztecan Language Family

Nahuatl is part of a very large language family called the Uto-Aztecan language family, a name that combines the Utes, up north in Utah, and Aztecan, referencing the Aztec/Mexicah empire. The family likely started around 4-5,000 years ago and is hypothesized to originate in the American Southwest, where it then split up in groups over time. The closest relatives to Nahuatl are Huichol (Wixarika) and Cora (Naayeri), who likely broke off at least 1,500 years ago, and which are still alive today. Pipil refers to a close relative to Huastecan Nahuatl, an endangered language in El Salvador.

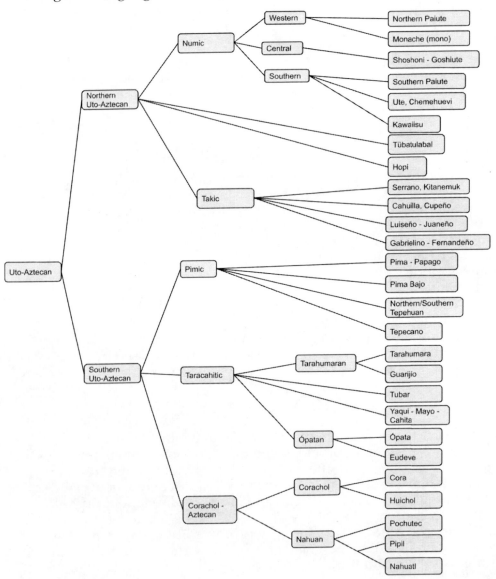

Regions of Nahuatl

Perhaps thanks to the Aztec empire and the Toltec empire before that, the Nahuatl language spread throughout Mexico, where it continues to be the most widely spoken native language, both geographically and numerically. With Spanish colonization, the Nahuatl regions lost more contact with each other, and today, it is not uncommon for Nahuatl speakers from different regions to use Spanish with each other when contact is made. These and other factors have led to fragmentation and isolation of many towns that have endured with the language. The Huasteca is unique in being such a large region that has maintained the language and culture alive. As mentioned, Huasteca Nahuatl is the largest variety of Nahuatl in terms of numbers of speakers, despite the seemingly small geographical range.

The map below groups together the major groups of Nahuatl varieties, but a few things should be noted. Firstly the division between groups can be arbitrary. One could divide the Huasteca in subgroups, though the variation is small. Secondly, not all towns or people within an outline will speak Nahuatl. The territory covered by the Central Nahuatl group is large as a whole, but it has relatively few speakers per square mile than the Huasteca, which would be much denser. Sayulteco Nahuatl went extinct since around the 1700s, and Jalisco-Colima Nahuatl recently went extinct between the 1970s and 1990s. Pipil Nahuatl is also severely endangered.

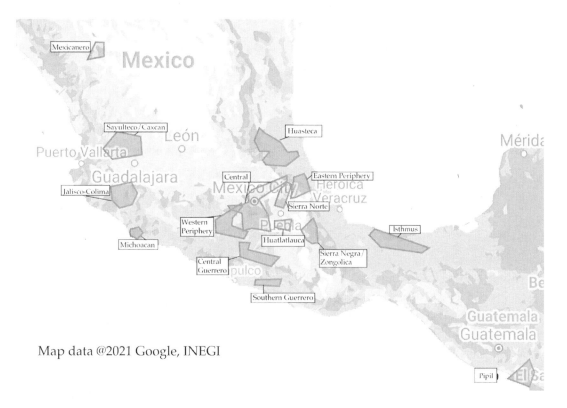

Map data @2021 Google, INEGI

1.

Pronunciation

Letter	Sound	Example	Meaning
a	a	atl	water
e	e	etl	bean
i	i	ichkatl	cotton
o	o	ohtli	road
p	p	pamitl	row
t	t	tokatl	spider
k	k	kakaoh	cacao
l	l	lemeni	It flames
m	m	tomin	money
n	n	nesi	It appears
h	h	ehekatl	wind
w	w	weyi	big
y	y	yayawik	black
s	s	se	one
ch	ch	chawistli	plague, aphids
x	sh	xoxoktik	green
ts	ts	tsapotl	sapote fruit
tl	tl	tlalli	land, earth
kw	kw	kwawitl	tree, stick

The vowels of Nahuatl are considered "pure" vowels, that is, they are similar to the vowels of Spanish (a, e, i, o). The pure vowel system is in fact, the most common way of pronouncing vowels across the world's languages, though it is not the only form. English, for example, has a tense/lax distinction that essentially doubles the amount of possible vowels, (consider: beat, bit, bet, bat, bought, boat, boot, butt).

Try to say: **noteco** "my lord". If it sounds like **no-te-kou**, you are making the vowels sound like English, instead, read it as if you were reading Spanish or Japanese: **no-te-ko**.

There is no /u/ sound in Nahuatl, sort of. In reality, both /o/ and /u/ are variations of the same sound, at least in the Nahuatl speaking mind. In fact, Nahuatl speakers learning Spanish often confuse words saying *borro* instead of *burro* (donkey), leading to discrimination by Spanish speakers.

Few varieties of Nahuatl prefer a /u/ pronunciation almost exclusively (Such as in El Salvador's Pipil language), though most varieties tend to use /o/. One reformed spelling system of Nahuatl uses /u/ as a consonant /w/, writing **ueyi** instead of **weyi**, for example. Ancient colonial Nahuatl, known as Classical Nahuatl, had this tendency as well, since Spanish had no letter /w/ in the 1500s.

Most consonants in Nahuatl sound the same as in Spanish and English, with an important difference in how Nahuatl /x/ sounds, which produces a -*sh*- sound, not a -*ks*- sound. This can lead to confusion for Spanish speaking learners, since Spanish has no -*sh*- sound, but only -*ch*-. This confusion is also why English speakers pronounce Mexico as *mek-si-kow*, while Nahuatl pronounces it as *me-shi-ko*.

Some letter combinations exist in Nahuatl, including /ch/, /sh/, /ts/, /kw/ and /tl/. The /ts/ sound is simply the combination of /t/ in front of /s/. This would be like pronouncing the /t/ in the word tsunami.

The trickiest sound for a non-native speaker is /tl/. This causes mispronunciation for both English and Spanish speakers since this sound does not exist in either of them (it is not the same as in Atlantis). You may find success by listening to native speakers for a long period first.

How to pronounce /tl/

Say the sound /l/ as in "long".
While keeping your tongue in this position, make the /h/ sound.
If the sound reminds you of a heavy lisp, you got it!
Now just add the /t/ in front of it, practice with **atl** "water".

Another consideration in Nahuatl writing is that two written /l/ don't make a /y/ sound like in Spanish spelling, they just make one /l/ sound. That is, **yollo** (heart) sounds like /yo-lo/.

There is some sound variation across different Nahuatl varieties. Central varieties tend to pronounce /w/, even when its at the end of a syllable, but the Huasteca varieties tend to pronounce it as /h/ at the end of a syllable. We continue to write /w/ so we can find the dictionary form, to maintain consistency and unification, and since it is a simple consistent pattern.

Central	Huasteca
To-na-tiw (sun)	To-na-tih (sun)
Nok-niw (my sibling)	No-ik-nih (my sibling)

Similarly, central varieties may continue to pronounce /kw/ even at the end of syllables, while the Huasteca simplifies this to /k/. Again, we write /kw/ to maintain consistency, and learn that it is really pronounced /k/.

Central	Huasteca
Nekw-tli (honey) Newk-tli (honey)	Nek-tli (honey)

In the Huasteca, when two /k/ sounds meet, it can sound like an /h/. Thus, you may see speakers write with an /h/, when it really is a /k/ sound. In fact, many syllable final consonants become an /h/ in the Huasteca. Observe these for consideration.

Huasteca Spelling	How it sounds	Meaning	Pattern
nikneki	nihneki	I want...	/kn/ > /hn/
nikkaki	nihkaki	I hear...	/kk/ > /hk/
kanin	kanih	Where?	Word final /n/ > /h/
mokawki	mokahki	It was left	Syllable final / w/ > /h/
Kitsakwki / kitsakki	kitsahki	He closed it	Syllable final /kw/ > /k/. Then /kk/ > /h/

Stress

Stress means the syllable which has the most emphasis in a word, it will generally be slightly louder, longer. Consider these English words to see the concept: english (éng-lish); computer (com-pú-ter); predictable (pre-díc-ta-ble); amazingly (a-má-zing-ly).

Nahuatl words have stress as well, but luckily this is a simple pattern, the second to last syllable always carries stress.

tlakwalli (food)	tla-kwál-li
teksistli (egg)	tek-sís-tli
chichi (dog)	chí-chi
notlakaw (my husband)	no-tlá-kah
nosiwaw (my wife)	no-sí-wah
tototl (bird)	tó-totl

Notice how /tl/ in **tototl** is part of the last syllable, but not its own syllable. A common mistake is to pronounce tototl as to-to-tuhl. Similarly the ancient deity Quetzalcoatl is often mispronounced as ke-tsal-kó-a-tuhl, instead of ke-tsal-kó-atl.

Keep in mind that each vowel in Nahuatl produces its own syllable, there are no diphthongs (sounds like ay, ey, ow, aw), at least not within the same syllable. See the following examples.

• Kokolia (to hate someone) - sounds like ko-ko-lí-a, not ko-kó-lya
• Mokokoa (to be sick) - sounds like mo-ko-kó-a, not mo-kó-kwa
• Koatl (ko-atl) - sounds like ko-atl, and not kwatl.

The difference between (ia) and (iya), as well as (oa) and (owa), can be quite difficult to hear, even for native speakers. In fact, there is no difference in their pronunciation for many speakers, who will interchange them in spelling. Often we will have to memorize the words, rather than rely on pronunciation, and the importance in this difference will be explored in a later chapter.

• **Nikkowa** - may be misspelled as *nihkoa*.
• **Nimotlaloa** - may be misspelled as *nimotlalowa*.
• **Tetiya** - may be misspelled as *tetia*.
• **Niktekiwia** - may be misspelled as *nijtekiwiya*.

Lastly, it is important to mention that vowels in Nahuatl may be short or long. However, this distinction only impacts few words and most spelling systems ignore this. Impacted words include **chichi** (dog/breasts); **tlatia** (to burn vs. to hide); **toka**(to plant/to follow).

Different Spelling Systems

The spelling system in this revised edition matches the modern spelling created through years of collaboration between native speakers, supported by a branch of the Mexican Government that gives some autonomy to indigenous language practices (INALI). This spelling is not pushed onto the communities by outside groups, academics or linguists, though it is hoped to be recognized by them in coming years.

The motive for redesigning spelling is multifaceted. For one, this spelling system reduces letter combinations invented by Spanish friars when the Spanish spelling system of the 1500s had to accommodate new sounds (such as w, ts, h, kw). The reduction of *hua* to *wa*, *cua* to *kwa*, *que* to *ke* saves space, but also provides for more consistency. Secondly, it is argued that it more closely parallels the letters with their actual pronunciation of Nahuatl, as native speakers argue that the letter /z/ should not be used as there is no /z/ sound in Nahuatl (though in reality any letter can be chosen to represent any sound for any alphabet, so long as the community understands it).

This change does bring one major disconnect, however, between Classical Nahuatl and Modern Nahuatl. With a change in spelling, native speakers will likely require more preparation before being able to read ancient Nahuatl texts. Nahuatl documents between the 1530s and the early 1800s are commonly called **Classical Nahuatl**. This actually reflects some variation across time and between regions, but it closely approximates the mainstream, lingua-franca Nahuatl that was used by the Aztec/Mexicah empire.

This change is not the first of its kind, however. Another branch of the Mexican government, called the SEP (Secretaria de Education Pública), produced a revised spelling in the 1940s under influence from the Christian linguistic organization named the Summer Institute of Linguistics (or SIL), and it continues to emphasize this system in school books. Even in the early 1900s, Nahuatl intellectuals learned about phonetics and exposure to linguistic methods and brought some of the first reforms to orthography, however it contained inconsistencies even among its users, and did not gain widespread attention. This is likely due to the fact that most Nahuatl speakers survived with an agricultural based society, which has lacked public education for over 400 years since the colonial period, and which thus has relatively few native speakers who know how to read and write. Most native speakers who are now learning to read and write reference Spanish spelling to help, but this is why native speakers are attempting to organize and create widespread reform.

Sound	Modern INALI	Classical	SEP	Spanish-based Spelling
kwa	kwa	cua	kua	cua
kwe	kwe	cue	kue	cue
kwi	kwi	cui	kui	cui
ka	ka	ca	ka	ca
ke	ke	que	ke	que
ki	ki	qui	ki	qui
ko	ko	co	ko	co
sa	sa	za	sa	sa
se	se	ce	se	se
si	si	ci	si	si
so	so	zo	so	so
wa	wa	hua	ua	ua / wa / hua
we	we	hue	ue	ue / we / hue
wi	wi	hui	ui	ui / wi / hui
h or '	h	h	j	j
ll	ll	ll	l	l
y	y	y	y	ll
x	x	x	x	sh

The simplified and modern INALI system will be used in this book.

The Classical system is not just one system, but a family of closely related systems, including the ACK system (commonly known as Andrews-Campbell-Karttunen Orthography), as well as the Jesuit order spelling, Horacio Carochi's system, Michel Launey's system and Una Canger's system. The Spanish-based spelling refers to the spelling used by native speakers whose only reference points are Spanish based orthographies.

Lastly, it is important to acknowledge that all these form of spelling are based on the Latin script, introduced by the Spanish clergy who wished to gain converts, while conquistadors were occupied with obtaining resources, land and labor. A native Nahuatl script based on pictographs and their correspondence to sounds was once used in pre-conquest times, with limited use in the early colonial period. However, this system did not capture all the sounds of Nahuatl, and was meant primarily for recording nouns, numbers, dates and names.

While no spelling system is 100% accepted among all native speakers, rather than spend energy on arguments, it will be most beneficial to learn to read them all.

For more help on pronouncing Nahuatl words, check or <u>Forvo.com</u>, the author has uploaded audio of over 1000 words. Furthermore, <u>Bible.is</u> has audio and text recordings in Nahuatl, though it is a Christian website. The Oregon Nahuatl dictionary has audio as well.

Exercise 1 — Try to read these words.

1. **Amo** - should sound like: A-mo

2. **Kena** - should sound like: KE-na

3. **Nanan** - should sound like: NA-nan

4. **Tetik** - should sound like: TE-tik

5. **Noyollo** - should sound like: no-YOL-lo

6. **Nonantsin** - should sound like: no-NAN-tsin

7. **Tlayi** - should sound like: TLA-yi (not KLA-yi)

8. **Awi** - should sound like: A-wi

9. **Siwatl** - should sound like: SI-watl

10. **Kwawitl** - should sound like: KWA-witl

11. **Tsahtsi** - should sound like: TSAH-tsi

12. **Ahwa** - should sound like: AH-wa

13. **Nekwtsin** - should sound like: NEK-tsin

14. **Mochiwtok** - should sound like: mo-CHIH-tok

Translations

amo	no	**siwatl**	woman
kena	yes	**kwawitl**	Tree, stick
nanan	mother	**tsahtsi**	To shout
tetik	Hard, strong	**ahwa**	To scold
noyollo	My heart	**nekwtsin**	honey
nonantsin	My mother	**mochiwtok**	it's made
tlayi	uncle	**awi**	aunt
tlaskamati	Thanks (Huasteca)	**tlasohkamati**	Thanks (Central)

2.

Plural Nouns

Let's start with nouns in Nahuatl. These include objects and people such as cats, dogs, girls, boys etc. You can tell something is a noun in Nahuatl because it will usually end with what is called an absolutive ending. The absolutive ending is important to recognize since it will disappear in many contexts. It will usually be either 'tli', 'tl', 'li' and in a few cases, 'n'. Below, I'll separate the noun from its absolutive ending/suffix.

Word	Breakdown	Meaning
koyotl	koyo-tl	coyote
amatl	ama-tl	paper
kamohtli	kamoh-tli	yam
pahtli	pah-tli	medicine
kalli	kal-li	house, structure
tamalli	tamal-li	tamal
sitlalin	sitlali-n	star
michin	michi-n	fish

Some nouns have no ending, especially borrowings.

Word	Breakdown	Meaning
miston	miston	cat
kawayoh	kawayoh	horse
patox	patox	duck

Recognizing the ending of a noun when you see it is the first step to modifying it. This absolutive ending will drop in many cases which we will see. The three forms of nouns are, simple, plural and possessed. The absolutive ending is only used in the simple cases, but is deleted in plurals and possession. Simple nouns in Nahuatl can be complete sentences, as there is no "BE/IS/ARE" verb in Huasteca Nahuatl.

Simple	Possessive	Plural
michin	*nomichin*	*michimeh*
fish /	my fish /	fish (plural) /
it's a fish	It's my fish	They are fish

Exercise 2 — Separate the root word from the absolute ending. The answers are in the back of this book.

1. Tlalli (land) _____

2. Nemilistli (life) _____

3. Siwapil (girl) _____

4. Kwapuertah (door) _____

5. Tepostli (metal) _____

6. Tlaltipaktli (world) _____

7. Amatl (paper) _____

8. Tlatsotsontli (music) _____

Now that you can split apart a word between its root and its absolutive ending, we can proceed to the main part of this chapter; making nouns plural. All we need to do is eliminate the absolutive ending and add -**meh**. This will make the difference between "cat" and "cats".

koyotl	coyote	**koyomeh**	coyotes
miston	cat	**mistonmeh**	cats
masewalli	person	**masewalmeh**	people
chichi	dog	**chichimeh**	dogs

Note that these examples are animate things, that is, they can move on their own. In Nahuatl, we don't pluralize words that are inanimate, for example, books, paper, houses, beds. However, the younger generation of Nahuatl speakers tends to pluralize more often, possibly from influence from Spanish. Thus, it's not wrong to say **amatl** 'papers' or **amameh** 'papers', it's just not common or necessary. Trees and plants have more animacy than obects, but not as much as animals and people. Thus, it's not uncommon to hear both **xochitl** and **xochimeh** for 'flowers'.

Exercise 3 — What does this mean? Use the word bank below to help.

1. Miston _____

2. Mistonmeh _____

3. Okwilimeh _____

4. Pantalon _____

5. Tototl _____

6. Tepetl _____

7. Amatl _____

Exercise 4 — How would you say...?

1. Women _____

2. Boys _____

3. Men _____

4. Fish(plural) _____

5. Dogs _____

6. Pigs _____

7. Indigenous people _____

8. Horses _____

9. Cities _____

10. Books _____

11. Snakes _____

miston	cat	**michin**	fish
tototl	bird	**pitsotl**	pig
amatl	paper	**kawayoh**	horse
okichpil	boy	**amoxtli**	book
okwilin	worm	**tepetl**	hill
siwatl	woman	**tlakatl**	man
chichi	dog	**masewalli**	indigenous person
altepetl	city, town	**koatl**	snake

Nouns With Numbers

Now that we can pluralize, add numbers before the noun to count.

se	1	**chikwase**	6
ome	2	**chikome**	7
eyi	3	**chikweyi**	8
nawi	4	**chiknawi**	9
makwilli	5	**mahtlaktli**	10

Se amoxtli

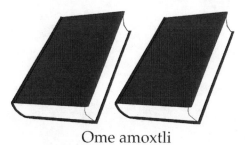

Ome amoxtli

Eyi amoxtli

Nawi amoxtli

Continue to 10 in your mind!

Noun Conjugation

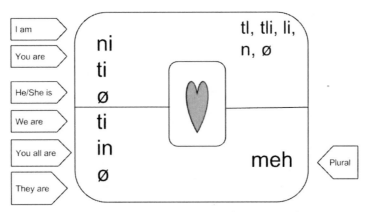

Using this Noun Conjugation chart, you have all the pieces necessary to say "I am a girl", "you are a boy", "she is a woman", etc. All we need to do is add a subject prefix, and if necessary, use the -meh plural ending we just learned of. **Tlakatl** means man, see the full conjugation of this noun. You should see the ø in the chart. This represents the lack of a sound, but which still marks the 3rd person. It's a silent placeholder. This means that just saying **tlakatl**, means both "man" and "He is a man".

- Nitlakatl   ni-tlaka-tl   I am a man
- Titlakatl   ti-tlaka-tl   You are a man
- Tlakatl   ø-tlaka-tl   He is a man
- Titlakameh   ti-tlaka-meh   We are men
- Intlakameh   in-tlaka-meh   You all are men
- Tlakameh   ø-tlaka-meh   They are men

Try to fill out the conjugation for siwatl 'woman'.

- I am a woman: _____
- You are a woman: _____
- She is a woman: _____
- We are women: _____
- You all are women: _____
- They are women: _____

I recommend saying the full conjugation of either "man" or "woman" out loud, a few times for several days. When you say "I am a woman" point to yourself. Same thing for "You are..." And "They are...". Modern Nahuatl does not have a word for other genders, but it does have words for other sexualities, such as **maxochitl** `gay male'.

For the following exercise, be careful with the word for "student". This word does not follow the same pattern for pluralization (adding -meh). We'll cover this scenario more in a later chapter. For now, just pay attention to the word bank.

Exercise 5 — How would you say...?

1. I am a teenage boy. _____

2. You are a teenage boy. _____

3. He is a teenage boy. _____

4. We are teenage boys. _____

5. You all are teenage boys. _____

6. They are teenage boys. _____

7. I am a teenage girl. _____

8. We are teenage girls. _____

9. They are teenage girls _____

10. He is a young boy. _____

11. They are young boys. _____

12. You are a young girl. _____

13. You all are young girls. _____

14. They are young girls. _____

15. I am a student. _____

16. You are a student. _____

17. She is a student. _____

18. They are students. _____

19. We are students. _____

20. You all are students. _____

telpokatl	teenage boy	ichpokatl	teenage girl
okichpil	young boy	momachtianih	students
siwapil	young girl	momachtihketl	student

Papalotl

Michin

Chichi

Ayotl

Tlen - What?

Inin - This   Inon - That

24

Conversation

Here's a conversation between a boy (okichpil) and his mother (inantsin). Use the translation text to help you understand the conversation.

Okichpil: Ma, inon se sayolin?

Inantsin: Amo

Okichpil: Tlen inon?

Inantsin: Inon se papalotl.

Okichpil: Inon papalotl weyi?

Inantsin: Amo, inon papalotl kwekwetstsin.

Okichpil: Namantsin nesih se, ome, eyi, nawi papalomeh!

Inantsin: Aah kena.

Okichpil: Ma, inin se miston?

Inantsin: Kena, inin se miston.

Okichpil: Inin miston weyi?

Inantsin: Amo, inin miston amo weyi.

Okichpil: Tlaskamati.

sayolin	A fly	**kena**	yes
kwekwetstsin	small	**amo**	no
weyi	big	**tlaskamati**	thanks
Ma	mom!	**namantsin**	now
nesih	appears		

Vocabulary: Domestic Animals

This subsection provides with bonus vocabulary, which will be important to develop our language skills as we continue. Many of these animals are considered to be **tlapiyalmeh**, or domesticated animals.

piyo	chicken	**chichi**	dog
wakax	cow	**miston**	cat
toroh	bull	**tototl**	bird
kwatochin	rabbit	**pitsotl**	pig

A **piyo** cannot fly very well, but a **tototl** can. You might see a **chichi** chase a **miston**. A **toroh** is male, but a **wakax** can be any gender. The **kwatochin** is an excellent runner, it must outrun **totomeh** such as eagles, owls, and hawks. A **pitsotl** stays cool in the mud.

Draw a **miston**	Draw a **chichi**	Draw a **tototl**

Draw a **wakax**	Draw a **piyo**	Draw a **toroh**

 Tlen inin?
_____

 Tlen inin?
_____

 Tlen inin?
_____

 Tlen inin?
_____

Tlapiyalmeh domestic animals

Across
2. chicken
4. cow
5. pig
7. dog
8. bull

Down
1. bird
3. rabbit
6. cat

3.

Possession

When we say "my shoe, your shoe, her shoe" we are saying we possess or have a relationship with a noun. To possess a noun in Nahuatl, you must once again eliminate the absolutive ending. After you've done this, you can add the prefix that tells you who the noun belongs to. For example;

- tekaktli - shoe
- notekak - my shoe
- It would be wrong to say 'tekak' by itself

You'll need to know the six possessive prefixes in Nahuatl that indicate who owns the item (it's mine, yours, her's, ours, theirs, of you all). Nahuatl is an agglutinating language–meaning that it's common for a word to be made up of many smaller pieces. In Nahuatl, the possessive prefixes attach to the front of the word. You can see the chart below contains the six prefixes in front of the word. To the right is a heart, **yollotl**. This represents the root of the word. So for the word notekak, **no** is the prefix which means 'my', and **tekak** `shoe' fits in the heart, or root of the word.

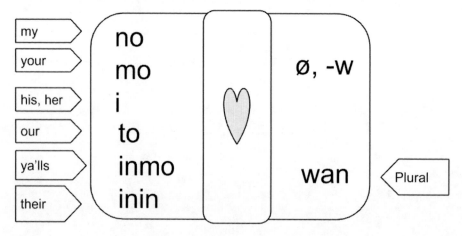

Chichi is 'dog', and **nochichi** means 'my dog.' But what if you have several dogs? In that case, you add the -**wan** at the end to pluralize the object. Can you guess how to say 'my dogs'? It's **nochichiwan**. Keep in mind, however, that inanimate objects are still not pluralized.

You should see and remember the ø in the chart. Most words drop the absolute ending when possessed, as we learned, and this symbol represents the lack of an absolutive ending, or any sound. For example, **yollotl** 'heart' becomes **no-yollo-ø**, 'my heart.'

Remember that a word can also be an entire sentence in Nahuatl. There is no word that means 'is', you just leave that blank. That means **nochichi** means 'my dog' and also means 'it is my dog'. By saying **nochichi** you are saying an entire sentence.

Exercise 6 — **Tlen kihtosneki?** What does this mean?

1. Nochichi _____

2. Nochichiwan _____

3. Motlayi _____

4. Motlayiwan_____

5. Noikniwan _____

6. Iikniwan _____

7. Toikniw _____

8. Inmoikniw _____

9. Ininikniw_____

10. Ininikniwan_____

11. Mokawayoh_____

12. Ininpitso _____

13. Motamal _____

14. Nokoton _____

15. Noew _____

16. Noaw _____

chichi	dog
tlayi	uncle
iknitl	sibling
kawayoh	horse
pitsotl	pig
tamalli	tamal
kotomitl	shirt
etl	beans
atl	water

Why the -w ?

Some objects take **-w** when possessed in the singular, particularly those that end in **-tl**. This includes **iknitl** 'sibling' which becomes **noikniw** 'my sibling'. Other examples are **noawakaw** 'my avocado', **noaw** 'my water'. As you can see, **-w** or ø can appear for the singular, but **-wan** must appear for the plural. To confirm, check a dictionary. Also remember word final -w is a soft /h/ in Huasteca Nahuatl.

Remember that nouns can be complete sentences. Thus, possessed nouns are not different. We can instantly apply this knowledge to begin introductions.

- **Notokah Juan** `My name is Juan'.

- **Motokah Mario** `Your name is Mario.'

- **Itokah Elena** `Her name is Elena.'

- **Keniwki motokah?** `What's your name?'

You can state someone's possession simply by using `i', which refers to `his' or `her'. This is equivalent to the [`s] in English, only here, we are literally saying `Maria her-dog'. There is no gender distinction in Nahuatl grammar.

- **Maria ichichi** `Maria's dog'

- **Ricardo inantsin** `Ricardo's mom'.

You can also use multiple possessed words in a sentence.

- **Maria inantsin ichichi** `Maria's mom's dog'

- **Ricardo itlayi ichan** `Ricardo's uncle's home'.

Irregular Possessives

A few nouns take a unique ending when possessed in the singular. These nouns end in **-wi**, likely a remnant of an ancient suffix. There are very few nouns that take this ending.

tlalli (land); **notlalwi** (my land)
pahtli (medicine); **nopahwi** (my medicine)
yeyohtli (daughter in law); **noyeyohwi** (my daughter in law)

Nouns that end in **-mitl** change to -**n**
Nouns that end in **-itl** change to **-h**.

kotomitl (shirt); **nokoton** (my shirt)
tokaitl (name); **notokah** (my name)
kweitl (skirt); **nokweh** (my skirt)

Greetings in the Huasteca, or most any Nahuatl communities, are much different than in English or Spanish, which tend to use greetings based on the time of day (good morning, good afternoon, etc). In Nahuatl communities, it is a custom to make statements to passerby's on the road as a form of acknowledgement. Typically, one states the obvious or your intentions (oh you're cutting weeds!, Oh you're resting! I'm going over there! We're going over there!). Polite greetings will be covered in a later section once we've developed the understanding to build those phrases.

Conversation

Lupeh: Piyali!

Lenoh: Piyali!

Lupeh: Keniwki motokah?

Lenoh: Notokah Lenoh, wan ta?

Lupeh: Na notokah Lupe.

Lenoh: Ah kwaltitok Lupe, nimitstlahpalos.

Lupeh: Nimitstlahpalos.

Lenoh: Lupe, tlen inon?

Lupeh: Inon nochichi.

Lenoh: Keniwki itokah mochichi?

Lupeh: Nochichi itokah Leon.

Lenoh: Ah kwaltitok.

piyali	hello, bye	**ta**	you
keniwki	how	**na**	I, me
tokaitl	name	**nimitstlahpalos**	I greet you
wan	and	**kwaltitok**	great

31

Exercise 7 — **Keniwki moillia?** How would you say...?

1. my tamal _____

2. It's my tamal _____

3. your uncle _____

4. their uncle_____

5. my shirt _____

6. my horses _____

7. our horses _____

8. your shirt _____

9. our dad_____

10. your (plural) mom_____

11. your aunt_____

12. she's your aunt _____

13. they are your aunts _____

atl	water	**etl**	beans
chichi	dog	**tlayi**	uncle
iknitl	sibling	**kawayoh**	horse
pitsotl	pig	**tamalli**	tamal
awitl	aunt	**kotomitl**	shirt
tatah	dad, father	**nanan**	mom, mother

Greetings in the Huasteca are done with a light touch of fingertips, not with a firm grasp.

nimitstlahpalos

Vocabulary: Face

Body part words must always be possessed. Generally speaking, you cannot say "foot" by itself.

notsontekon	my head	**notsonkal**	my hair
noixtiyol	my eye	**noyakatsol**	my nose
nonakas	my ears	**noixxayak**	my face

Label the parts of his face. Remember -i- means his/hers.

Match

1. motsontekon ___   (a) your mouth

2. moixtiyol ___   (b) your nose

3. mokamak ___   (c) your head

4. moyakatsol ___   (d) your ears

5. monakas ___   (e) your eye

Tson-

One of the tricks that will make learning Nahuatl easier is to notice the patterns, the small particles that will appear over and over. In this set, you may have noticed the particle -**tson**- appear twice. -**Tson** typically refers to the top part of a person's body, often around the head, while **tsin-** refers to the base, bottom, or butt.

4.

Introduction to Verbs

By now we've seen some short sentences without using any verbs, or action words. In this chapter, we'll begin to explore the basics of how verbs work in Nahuatl. Verbs are really the backbone to any language, and they are generally the most complicated aspect. By understanding how Nahuatl puts together pieces (morphemes), you can start to break down any word and see patterns of changes in other varieties.
The prefixes for verbs go in front of the word's root, its heart: **iyollo**.

Using the chart below, try to make sense of these examples. This chart only applies to verbs.

Niwitoni	I jump
Tiwitoni	You jump
Witoni	He/She/It jumps
Tiwitonih	We jump
Inwitonih	Ya'll jump
Witonih	They jump

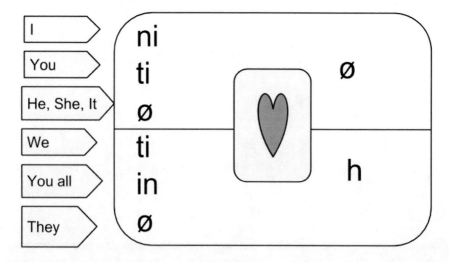

Perhaps you figured out that **ni** means `I' and **witoni** means to jump. There is nothing that goes at the end of the verb when it's singular and present tense, we indicate this with the /Ø/, but when it's plural, it needs to have an /h/. As you might be able to see, the difference between **witoni** `she jumps' and **witonih** `they jump' is very small.

It's also important to note that the third person singular and plural have no subject prefix. By third person, I'm referring to actions done by `him, her, it, they.' This means that the root word by itself is already in the third person. For example, **witoni** by itself can mean `he, she, it jumps.'

Lastly, Nahuatl verbs don't care about gender. Whether `he' does an action or `she' does it, it will still always have the same form. In other words, there is no difference between `he runs' and `she runs.'

At this point, it might be helpful to say all the conjugations of `jump' and visualize them in your head while you say them out loud.

Exercise 8 — **Keniwki moillia?** How would you say...?

1. I am sick_____

2. You are sick _____

3. He is sick_____

4. We are sick_____

5. You all are sick _____

6. They are sick _____

7. I'm eating _____

8. You are eating _____

9. She is eating_____

10. We are eating_____

11. You all are eating_____

12. They are eating _____

13. I am running _____

14. I am studying _____

15. They are studying _____

tlakwa	to eat	motlaloa	to run
momachtia	to study	mokokoa	to be sick

Independent Pronouns

Simply by saying **witoni** we mean that `she runs'. However, it is also possible to add in the independent pronouns and still get the same meaning. By independent pronoun, I mean a pronoun that is not attached to the root word and is optional. (If you are familiar with Spanish, you can see the same parallel with the phrase `ella camina' vs. `camina.' They both mean the same thing, only the first one has the independent pronoun `ella,' which is optional.)

Na	I, me
Ta	You
Ya	He, She, It
Tohwantin	Us
Inmohwantin	You all
Inihwantin/ Yahwantin	They

These pronouns can imply a subject or object, there is no difference between "I" and "Me" with these pronouns. For example, if someone were to ask "who is going to the store?", you can respond with "**na!**" (me!). And if someone asks, "who got hurt?", you would still use the same form "**na!**". Also, you can use the independent pronouns with a verb to emphasize who does the action. Keep in mind, the independent pronouns are optional.

Na niwitoni   I am jumping.

Ta tiyas   YOU are going.

Can you state why this sentence is incorrect?

*Na tlakwa. I eat.

This is because it still requires the prefix **ni**, it should be **Na nitlakwa** or just **Nitlakwa**.

In most central Nahuatl towns, but rarely in the Huasteca, you can add respect by adding -tzin to the end of the pronoun `you'. These towns say **Tehwatl** or **tehwa** or **teh** (you), and **Tehwatsin** (you, with respect). **Ta** in the Huasteca is a simplified, but related version of **tehwatl**. A few central towns also preserve an ancient word **Momawisotsin** `Your reverence'.

Exercise 9 — **Tlen kihtosneki?**

1. Na nitlakwa_____

2. Ya momachtia _____

3. Tohwantin timotlaloah_____

4. Intlakwah_____

5. Nehnemi_____

6. Inihhwantin nehnemih_____

7. Mohmostla nikochi_____

8. Ta titlahkwiloa_____

9. Kemmantsin titlahkwiloah_____

10. Inmomachtiah_____

11. Tohwantin timomachtiah_____

Exercise 10 — **Keniwki moillia? (note, two possible ways)**

1. I am eating_____

2. You are eating _____

3. We are eating_____

4. I am walking_____

5. We are walking_____

6. She is running_____

7. He is writing_____

8. You all are eating_____

9. We are running_____

10. They are studying_____

11. He is studying_____

12. I am studying _____

13. You sleep everyday _____

14. We sleep everyday _____

15. I sometimes study _____

tlakwa	to eat	**motlaloa**	to run
momachtia	to study	**nehnemi**	to walk
kochi	to sleep	**tlahkwiloa**	to write
mohmostla	every day	**kemmantsin**	sometimes

Tsin- Little/Respect

-Tsin is a suffix that can imply "little" and/or respect. The meaning depends on how you imply it in context. We first observed this with the word **tehwatsin** `you', used in some regions. Note, however, this -**tsin** suffix is different from the **tsin-** prefix used in body parts, and which can imply something's base or bottom. The absolutive ending of nouns is once again dropped.

etl   beans

etsin   little beans (respectfully)

atsin   little water (respectfully)

konetsin   little child (may not imply respect)

Juantsin   little Juan (implies respect).

A second, related prefix is -pil, which also gives connotations of smallness. When used in combination with -tsin, it can further exaggerate the smallness or respect.

piletsin   sacred beans

pilatsin   sacred water

pilkonetsin   baby infant

pilchichitsin   baby puppy

Ancient and Central Nahuatl varieties may also use other suffixes with nouns. In their towns, -**ton** implies smallness just like -**tsin**, only respect is not implied. Lastly, in these towns, the suffix -**pol** can mean wretched, big.

To pluralize a word ending in -**tsin**, you reduplicate so it becomes -**tsitsin**.

konetsitsin (children)

Vocabulary: Earth

We'll wrap up this section with more vocabulary. Note these are words are nouns, as given away by their endings.

kwawitl	tree, stick, wood	sakatl	grass, hay
tepetl	hill	ohtli	road
tetl	rock	xalli	sand
tlasolli	trash	tlalli	land,
xiwitl	plant; year	weyi atl	lake, river, ocean
xochitl	flower	sokitl	mud

Totlaltikpak: Our world

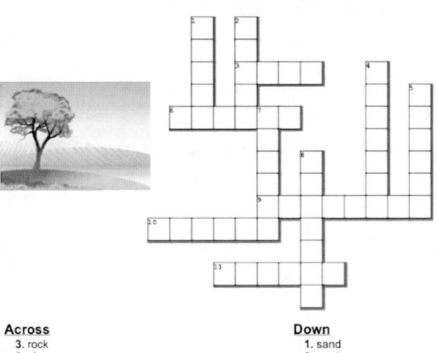

Across
3. rock
6. plant
9. trash
10. mud
11. grass

Down
1. sand
2. road
4. flower
5. land
7. hill
8. tree, stick

5.

Commands

Whenever we request someone to do an action, or say what should happen, we usually use an imperative, a command. For example `go away', `eat your food', or `help me!'. In Nahuatl, you simply need to add xi- in front of the root verb to make it a command, and delete -a from any verb that ends in -ia or -oa. Keep in mind the stress will shift, since you deleted a vowel and syllable, the stress will once again return to the second-to-last syllable. (stress written here for demonstration)

tlákwa (to eat) --> **xitlákwa!** Eat!

motlalóa (to run) --> **ximotlálo!** Run!

momachtía (to study) --> **ximomáchti!** Study!

If you make a command to two or several people, you need to add the plural suffix -**kan**.

Xitlakwakan! You all eat!

Ximotlalokan! You all run!

Ximomachtikan! You all study!

There is no word that means `please'. You will find many words and concepts from English don't exist in Nahuatl, and this is typical as you encounter a new language. Using the command form on verbs is not considered rude, unless the context implies it. One way to soften a command is to add the prefix -**on**- right before the root. -**on**- implies `quickly', `right away', or `towards there'. A second way is to add the word **welis** which means "is it possible? could you?".

Xiontlakwa. Go eat. (soft request)

Xionmomachti. Go study (soft request)

Welis ximotlalo? Could you go run?

In western varieties of Nahuatl (as in the state of Guerrero), it is the norm to reduce -xi- and just say -x- when speaking fast. For example, **xitlakwa** can be said **xtlakwa**, and **xionmomachti** can be **xonmomachti**.

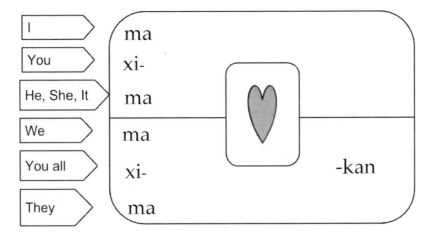

Remember there are six grammatical pronouns in Nahuatl (I, you, she, us, you all, they). So far, we've learned how to make commands for "you" and "you all", but we need to know how to make commands for the rest. "You" and "You all" are direct commands, which uses a different system than the rest.

Any non-direct commands will use the particle **ma**.

Ma nikochi   I should sleep

Ma kochi   He needs to sleep

Ma tikochikan   Let's go to sleep

Ma kochikan   They need to sleep.

Some varieties can use both **ma** and **xi-** together, in which case the command is softened. This does not make sense in Huasteca Nahuatl, however.

Ma xiwallaw   Come here please.

Note that commands are used to indicate when someone makes a request, or wishes something. This includes some cases in English where the verb uses the infinitive, which does not exist in Nahuatl, and which instead uses the command tense. See these examples: (**kineki** means `he or she wants').

Kineki ma nikochi   She wants me <u>to sleep</u>.

However, the command is not necessary where there is no imperative meaning.

Nikneki nikochis (I want to sleep).

41

Exercise 11 — **Tlen kihtosneki?**

1. Ma niyaw_____
2. Xiyaw _____
3. Ma yowi_____
4. Ma tiyakan_____
5. Xiwallaw_____
6. Xiwallakan_____
7. Xichoka_____
8. Xikochikan_____
9. Ma tlaawetsi_____
10. Xisanilo_____
11. Ma ihsa_____
12. Ma titlakwakan_____

Exercise 12 — **Keniwki moillia?**

1. Let's dance!_____
2. You dance! _____
3. Sing!_____
4. You all sing!_____
5. Let's sing!_____
6. Wake up! _____
7. They should sing!_____
8. He says she should sleep!_____
9. Eat!_____
10. You all eat! _____
11. May it be sunny! _____

tlakwa	to eat	**kihtoa**	he/she says
choka	to cry	**motlaloa**	to run
mihtotia	to dance	**tlaawetsi**	to rain
wika	to sing	**saniloa**	to speak
ihsa	to wake up	**tona**	to be sunny
ya/yaw	to go	**walla/wallaw**	to come

Irregular Verbs

Now that we've seen some verbs, it's important to be aware of irregular patterns in verbs; conjugations that don't follow the pattern. Luckily, there are only two major irregular verbs in Huasteca Nahuatl: to go and to come. **Yaw** changes to **Yowi** starting with the third person singular. **Wallaw** changes to **Wallowi** in all the plural forms.

Niyaw	I go	**Niwallaw**	I come
Tiyaw	You go	**Tiwallaw**	You come
Yowi	He/she goes	**Wallaw**	She/he comes
Tiyowih	We go	**Tiwallowih**	We come
Inyowih	You all go	**Inwallowih**	You all come
Yowih	They go	**Wallowih**	They come

In commands, the base form for singulars is **-yaw-** and **-wallaw-**, while the plural command forms are **-ya-** and **-walla-**. In most other tenses, the base form is **-ya-** and **-walla-**.

Ma niyaw	I should go	**Ma niwallaw**	I should come
Xiyaw	You should go	**Xiwallaw**	You should come
Ma yaw	He should go	**Ma wallaw**	She should come
Ma tiyakan	Let's go	**Ma tiwallakan**	We should come
Xiyakan	You all should go	**Xiwallakan**	You all should come
Ma yakan	They should go	**Ma wallakan**	They should come

Irregular patterns are often remnants of an ancient system that was replaced in a language, similar to the changes in "eat vs. ate" in English. In Nahuatl the ancient form is likely **yowi/yawi,** and **wallowi** which were simplified.

Vocabulary: Places

kwatenno	bathroom (the edge of the trees)	**weyi altepetl**	city
tiankis	market	**chinanko**	neighborhood, village
kwatitlan	forest; in the forest	**kalli**	building, house
nochan	my home	**tiopan**	church
millah	at the corn field	**kalihtik**	inside
altepetl	town	**kaltenno**	outside, by the home's edge

Prepositions in Nahuatl are often suffixes, instead of standalone words. There are several prepositional suffixes (-tlan, -tlah -pan, -ko/-no) which will be covered in coming sections. For now, just be aware some words like **kwatitlan** can mean both `forest' and `at the forest'.

Match

1. kwatenno ___
2. tiankis ___
3. kwatitlan ___
4. nochan ___
5. millah ___
6. altepetl ___
7. weyi altepetl ___
8. chinanko ___
9. kalli ___
10. tiopan ___
11. kalihtik ___

(a) bathroom
(b) building, house
(c) my home
(d) church
(e) city
(f) town
(g) forest
(h) neighborhood
(i) corn field
(j) market
(k) inside a building

Homes in the Huasteca were traditionally palm hut homes, but were pressured by the government to adopt metal-based roofs in order to be given electrical access.

6.

To BE, To Exist

Eli

As previously mentioned, there is no copula `BE' verb in Nahuatl to indicate words such as `I <u>am</u> a student'. Instead, one simply adds a prefix (such as **ni-**, I am) onto the word `student' to produce **nimomachtihketl**.

However, there are ways in Huasteca Nahuatl to state you `were', `will be' or `would be' a student. Huasteca Nahuatl is unique in using the verb **eli**, which means `to become', among other things.

> **eliyaya** - used to be (for a period of time)

> **elki** - was (but stopped)

> **elis** - will be

> **eliskia** - would be

You can now combine the subject prefixes with **-eli-** to make countless combinations. A subject prefix is required on both the verb and the noun.

> **Nieliyaya nikonetl.** - I used to be a child.

> **Nielki nikonetl.** - I was a child.

> **Nielis nimomachtihketl.** - I will be a student.

> **Nieliskia nimomachtihketl.** - I would be a student.

> **Nimomachtihketl** - I am a student.

> (not)   ***Nieli nomachtihketl** - I am a student

Central varieties of Nahuatl use -ye- instead of -eli to link `BE' with a noun.

> **Niyes nixinachtli** - I will be a seed.

Itstok/Eltok

The verb "To be present", such as in "I'm here", "Is she there?", "Jorge is not present", works much different from English, and also varies by region. In Classical and Central Nahuatl varieties, the common `be' verb is **ka** in the singular, and **kateh** in the plural.

Nikan nika - Here I am.

Nikan tikateh - Here we are.

The Huasteca works differently. It makes a distinction between whether something is animate (moves on its own) or inanimate (is stationary). Animate entities use the verb **itstok** while inanimates use **eltok**. These more or less mean "to be present". These have a plural form as **itstokeh** and **eltokeh**.

Nikan niitstok. - Here I am.

Nikan tiitstokeh. - Here we are.

Nikan eltok se amoxtli. - Here is a book.

Kanin itstok Juan? - Where is Juan?

Kanin eltok mochan? - Where is your home?

Remember again that **itstok/eltok** imply being present. It is common for one to produce the following errors, caused by translating "is/are" as **itstok**.

Not: ***Niitstok nimokokoa** - I am sick

Correct: **Nimokokoa** - I am sick (literally I + BE + sick)

Correct: **Nikan niitstok** - I am here (literally I + present)

Onkah

The Huasteca does use a form similar to the Central **ka**, which is **onkah**. In nearly all regions, **onkah** means "exist, there are". `To exist ' is different from `to be present', as something can exist without being present in your space in that moment. Here are some examples.

Onkah chichimeh. - There are dogs.

Onkah tepahtianih. - There are doctors.

To be present (animate)	To be present (inanimate)	To exist, there are
Itstok se kawayoh. `There's a horse present.'	**Eltok** se amatl. `There's a paper present.'	**Onkah** amatl. `There are papers.' (exist)
Axitstok `He's not here' (present)	**Axeltok** (They exist but it's not here)	**Axonkah** (There's none)

Exercise 13 — **Tlen kihtosneki?**

1. Itstok Maria_____

2. Axkanah Itstok Maria _____

3. Eltok se amatl_____

4. Itstok nochichi_____

5. Eltok nochan_____

6. Itstok se tlakatl_____

7. Axonkah atl_____

8. Onkah tlakwalli?_____

Exercise 14 — **Keniwki moillia?**

1. Is she here?_____

2. Is it here?_____

3. Here is a chair._____

4. Here are two chairs._____

5. The chair is not here._____

6. There are no chairs._____

7. There's no problem._____

8. Is there a question?_____

9. There's work. _____

10. Here is a bed. _____

amatl	paper	**chichi**	dog
tlakatl	man	**tlakwalli**	food
atl	water	**kwasiyah**	chair
chantli	home	**tlahtlanilistli**	question
tekitl	work	**tlapechtli**	bed
axkanah	no, not		

Negation

Negation in Nahuatl can be expressed in two ways: using a negative word, or using a negative prefix. Axkanah is a unique form of 'no' only in the Huasteca. Most regions use **amo** instead of **axkanah**. Since Huasteca has both, amo can be a stronger `no', used especially in negative commands.

amo	no, not	**amokanah**	no, not
axkanah	no, not	**ax-**	no not
axakah	no one	**axikah**	nowhere
ayikana	not yet	**ayi-**	not yet
ayokkana	no longer, not anymore	**ayok-**	no longer
amo tlen	nothing	**axtlen**	nothing

These negative words and prefixes can attach to many things such as verbs, adjectives, and nouns.

Amo nisiwapil, niichpokatl. I'm not a little girl, I'm a teenage girl.

Axniokichpil, nitelpokatl. I'm not a little boy, I'm a teenage boy.

Ayikana nisiwatl. I'm not a woman yet.

Ayokkana niokichpil. I'm not a little boy anymore.

Axitstok Juan. Juan isn't present.

Axonkah nakatl. There's no meat.

Axweyi nochan. My home's not big.

Amo xiyaw. Don't go.

Axxiyaw. Don't go.

Ma amo tona. May it not be sunny.

Classical Nahuatl used **ah-** in the same way and meaning as **ax-**.

ahkwalli - not good.

Central varieties also use makamo to negate commands.

Makamo xiyaw. Don't go.

Vocabulary: Objects

amoxtli	book	**tepostli**	metal
amatl	paper	**tepostlahkwilolli**	computer (metal writing)
tlikolli	pen, pencil, ink	**tepostototl**	plane (metal bird)
kwamesah	wooden table	**tepostokatsawalli**	internet (metal spider web)
kwasiyah	wooden chair	**tlawilli**	light
kwapuertah	wooden door	**pilxalohtsin**	mug, cup
tomin	money	**tlakemitl**	blanket

Across
3. flies in the sky
7. lets you see in the dark
8. Tool for writing with

Down
1. Tool for writing on
2. Tool for reading
4. covers you in the cold
5. Thing with which you buy
6. strong compound from minerals

Here and There, This and That

Taking into account our knowledge of **itstok** and **eltok** (to be present), we can combine these with the words for `here' and `there' to make new sentences.

nikan - here

nopayoh - there (by the listener)

neka - way over there (out of sight)

nepa - way over there (in sight)

kakaahko - up there

kakatlani - down there

Nopayoh is only in the Huasteca, and it can also be pronounced **nopayah**, or **nopona**. Central varieties say **ompa**.

Here are other important demonstratives. There's several synonyms. Remember these /w/ sound like an /h/ since they are syllable final. Though it may seem like a lot of variation, note the patterns.

inin	this	**inon**	that
ni	this	**ne**	that
iwki	like so	**nopa**	that
iwkinin	like this	**iwkinon**	like that
kenni	like this	**kenne**	like that
kewkinin	like this	**kewkinon**	like that
		kennopa	like that

All the variation can be explained when you consider the pieces. The root forms for "this" are **inin** and **ni**. The word **iwki** means like `like so', **ken** means `like' and **kew** is likely a simplification of **keniwki** `how'. This process is repeated with the words that mean `that'.

By now you may have noticed there's no word that means `the', as in `the boy', you simply say `boy'. However, it's common to use **inon/ne/ nopa** in a similar way to `the' or `that'.

ne okichpil kochis   the boy will sleep / that boy will sleep

Vocabulary: Common Adverbs

yolik	slow	**chikawak**	hard, fast
senkah	same	**nochi**	all, everyone
nowkiya	also	**no**	also
naman	now, today	**niman**	soon
nechka	close by	**wahka**	far away
namantsin	right now	**nimantsin**	very soon
sehsen	each and every one	**san**	just
sampa	again	**seyok**	next
tlawel	very	**cheneh**	too much
pani	too much	**eheliwis**	all over
owih	difficult	**axowih**	not difficult

Examples

1. **Tlawel nimayana.** - I'm very hungry.
2. **Nimantsin niyaw.** - I'm going soon.
3. **Sehsen ichpokatl kipiyas iamox.** - Each girl will have a book.
4. **Cheneh owih ni tekitl.** - This task is too hard.
5. **Yolik xikihto.** - Could you say it slowly?
6. **Sampa xikihto.** - Could you say it again?
7. **Ne amoxtli wan ni amoxtli senkah.** - This and that book are the same.
8. **Seyok amatl.** - Next page.
9. **Nonechka xinehnemi.** - Walk close to me.
10. **Nowahka xinehnemi.** - Walk far from me.

Adverbs

Complete the crossword puzzle below

<u>Across</u>
1. just
3. very
8. fast, hard
9. difficult

<u>Down</u>
1. again
2. same
4. all
5. soon
6. today
7. slow

Determiner or Pronoun?

Determiners can go before a noun, but a pronoun take the place of the noun.

some cats swim   some swim
(determiner)   (pronoun)

See the examples below to view these in Nahuatl. The form ending with `eh' are simply plural forms. This includes **seyok** > **seyokeh** and **sekinok** > **sekinokeh**.

Determiner   Pronoun

Determiner
nochi - all
miak - many
sekin - some
seyok - another
sekinok - another (different)

Pronoun
nochimeh - everyone
miak/miakin - many
sekin - some
seyok/seyokeh - another, others
sekinok/sekinokeh - others (different)

Nochi chichimeh motlaloah
All the dogs run.

Nochimeh motlaloah
Everyone runs.

Miak chichimeh motlaloah
Many dogs run.

Miakin motlaloah
Many run.

Sekin chichimh motlaloah
Som dogs run.

Sekin motlaloah
Some run.

Seyok chichi motlaloa
Another (one more) dog runs.

Seyokeh Motlaloah.
Others run.

Sekinok chichi motlaloa.
Another (different) dog runs.

Sekinokeh motlaloa.
Others run.

The plural forms **nochimeh** and **miakin** only exist as pronouns, meaning they cannot be used directly with nouns.

*Nochimeh chichimeh motlaloah.
*Miakin chichimeh motlaloah.

Vocabulary: Deities

The reader familiar with the Aztec pantheon might be surprised to know that modern Nahuatl communities don't recognize ancient Aztec/Mexicah deities such as Huitzilopochtli or Tezcatl Ipoca, save for a few towns in Puebla that still give offerings to Tlaloc. This may be because of colonization, christianity, as well as the fact that different communities likely gave offerings to different deities even in ancient times. Still, modern Huasteca communities continue to perform ancient ceremonies most relevant to everyday life, such as rain and cleansing ceremonies. Payments and offerings to the spirits continue to involve blood sacrifice of small animals. The emphasis on spirituality continues to play an important role in native communities. Below are some of the most prevalent vocabulary.

kampeka	a ritual, ceremony	**Tlatektli**	paper cuttings that represent spirits. They are treated as living objects and fed blood.
malwilli	any sacred object, can be dangerous and must be treated with utmost respect	**Totekoh**	our lord, refers to God
tepatihketl	a healer, shaman or doctor	**Totiotsin**	same as teotl, refers to spirit deities
tetiochiwketl	shaman in charge of burial ceremonies	**Ehekatl**	the wind spirit, considered evil
tetlachiwketl	shaman of dark spells	**Awahkeh**	rain deities
totahtsin	christian priest	**Tlakatekolotl**	demon-like spirit
xochitlalketl	shaman in charge of certain ceremonies	**Tlawelilok**	demon-like spirit
tlaixpan	altar	**Tonantsin**	Virgin of Guadalupe
tlamanalistli	harvest ceremony	**Chikomexochitl**	sacred boy and girl who brought the corn
tlatlakwaltiah	feeding spirits ceremony	**Apanchaneh**	mermaid, has relationship to rain
tlawentilistli	cleansing curses ceremony		

7.

Future Tense

We've learned how to manipulate verbs in basic ways using different prefixes. Another way to manipulate verbs is by changing the tense, which will use suffixes in Nahuatl. Thus, we can express a verb in future tense (I will sleep), present tense (I sleep), past tense (I slept) or the conditional tense (I would sleep if I could). We technically reviewed present tense already, its the default tense when you use a base verb (**niwitoni**: I jump, I am jumping). In this chapter, we'll start with another simple tense, the future.

For the future tense, we simply add the suffix **-s** to the end of the root if the subject prefix is singular. If the subject is plural then we add the suffix **-seh**.

Nikochis	I will sleep
Tikochis	You will sleep
Kochis	She will sleep
Tikochiseh	We will sleep
Inkochiseh	Ya'll will sleep
Kochiseh	They will sleep

Before we can add the **-s**, we must also delete the final /**a**/ in words that end in **-ia** or **-oa**.

Nimokwesoa	I am sad
Nimokwesos	I will be sad
Timokwesos	You will be sad
Mokwesos	He will be sad
Timokwesoseh	We will be sad
Inmokwesoseh	You all will be sad
Mokwesoseh	They will be sad

Here's another example with a verb that ends in **-ia**.

Nimihtotia	I dance/I am dancing
Nimihtotis	I will dance
Timihtotis	You will dance
Mihtotis	He will dance
Timihtotiseh	We will dance
Inmihtotiseh	You all will dance
Mihtotiseh	They will dance

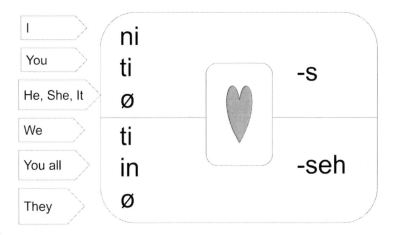

Exercise 15 — **Tlen kihtosneki?**

1. Nikochis tlayowa_____

2. Amo kochiseh_____

3. Axkanah timihtotiseh_____

4. Mostla amo tlaawetsis_____

5. Ayikana nitlakwas._____

6. Ayokkana nimihtotis._____

7. Axakah wikas._____

8. Tiwikaseh senyowal._____

9. Amo tiwikas mostla. _____

10. Ayoktichokaseh. _____

kochi	to sleep	mostla	tomorrow
tlayowa	at night	tlakwa	to eat
wika	to sing	senyowal	all night

Central and Classical Nahuatl use -skeh for the future plural.
(timihtotiskeh: we will dance).

Exercise 16 — **Keniwki moillia?**

1. Tomorrow I'll sleep._____

2. Tomorrow we will run._____

3. It's going to rain all night._____

4. You will sleep at night._____

5. You won't sleep all night._____

6. We will dance all night.._____

7. We will speak tomorrow._____

8. They will wake up tomorrow._____

9. I will run tomorrow._____

10. I won't eat tomorrow. _____

11. The moon will shine all night. _____

12. The moon won't shine at night. _____

metstona	for the moon to shine	**ihsa**	to wake up
tlayowa	at night	**saniloa**	to speak
senyowal	all night	**tlaawetsi**	to rain

Vocabulary: Questions

In Nahuatl, a few question words have two versions, one used in statements and one for questions.

kanin? / kanke?	where?	**kampa**	where
kenke? / tleika?	why?	**pampa**	because
akkiya?	who?	**tlen/anke**	he who; she who; those who

Both **tlen** and **anke** are interchangeable, although **tlen** is most common. **Axanke** is commonly used to mean `no one'.

Kanin itstok nochichi. **Where** is my dog?

Itstok kampa alaxoxkwawitl. He's **where** the orange tree is.

Careful, these sentences below are statements yet they use the question forms. One way to tell apart the differences is to interpret **akkiya** as `who' and **tlen/anke** as `he who, she who, those who'. Another way is to consider that the question forms are also used to begin a subordinate clause.

Axnikmati <u>akkiya</u> wallas.	I don't know <u>who</u> will come.
Kena nikmati akkiya elis tepahtihketl.	I DO know <u>who</u> will be a doctor.
Wallas <u>tlen</u> wika.	<u>He who</u> sings is coming.
Nikmati kanin eltok momorral.	I know <u>where</u> your bag is.
Eltok kampa kwamesah.	It's <u>where</u> the table (is).

Most other question words are straightforward.

kanin? / kanke?	where?	**kanin tikochis?**	Where will you sleep?
kenke?	why?	**kenke tiyas?**	Why are you going?
tleika?	why?	**Tleika tiyas?**	Why are you going?
akkiya?	who?	**Akkiya yas?**	Who is going?
kemman?	when?	**Kemman tiyas?**	When are you going?
tlen?	what?	**Tlen tikneki?**	What do you want?
keniwki?	how?	**Keniwki moillia?**	How is it said?
keniwkatsa?	in what way?	**Keniwkatsa mochiwa?**	How is it done?
kemmaniwki?	when exactly?	**Kemmaniwki tiyaseh?**	When exactly are we going?
keski?	how many?	**Keski tikneki?**	How many do you want?
katlinya?	which one?	**Katlinya tikneki?**	Which one do you want?

Using Two Verbs

Consider sentences where you use two verbs, like in saying "I want to dance" or "I like to dance". Consider the following attempts to say "I want to dance", given that **nikneki** is `I want' and **mihtotia** is `to dance'.

A. *Nikneki mihtotia

B. *Nikneki nimihtotia

C. *Nikneki mihtotis

D. Nikneki nimihtotis

Beginners often make mistakes on sentences like these, but it is also easy to overcome. Answer (A) is not correct, this would sound like you're saying "I want he is dancing". Remember that mihtotia can mean `to dance', but it also means `he is dancing'. Answer (B) is not incorrect, but it less common, this would sound something like `I want to be dancing'. (C) is wrong as well, it means "I want that he will dance", so it makes the same mistake as (A). (D) is the correct form, but why? Both verbs need to agree with each other in terms of the pronouns. A literal translation in English would be `I+want I+will.dance'. Though it may appear redundant, it is necessary in Nahuatl.

Why is (D) preferred over (B)? This is because when you say `TO' in `TO dance', you are implying dancing is a possibility in the future, and not that someone is dancing right now. It's the same when you say `I like to dance'. You are not saying `I like that I am dancing right now', you are saying that you like the possibility of you dancing, and for a Nahuatl speaker this implies the future. Here's more examples.

Nikneki nikochis	I want to sleep
Tikneki tikochis	You want to sleep
Kineki kochis	She wants to sleep
Tiknekih tikochiseh	We want to sleep
Axtikneki tikochis?	Don't you want to sleep?
Nikneki nitlakwas	I want to eat

We can combine the lessons in this section to produce new sentences like these.

Kanin tikochis?	Where will you sleep?
Kenke tikochis?	Why will you sleep?
Akkiya kochis?	Who will sleep?
Nikochis kampa nochan.	I will sleep where my home is.
Nikochis pampa nimokwesoa.	I will sleep because I'm sad.
Kochiseh tlen mokwesoah.	The tired ones will sleep.

With: Ika and Wanya

Both **ika** and **wanya** translate to `with', but they are used in different circumstances. **Ika** is used as an instrumental case to state that an action was done with the help of a tool. **Wanya** is used to state that an action was done together with another person or thing. A simple method is to consider **ika** to mean `with' and **wanya** to mean `together with'.

Nitlakwas ika tlaxkalli.	I'm going to eat with a tortilla.
Nitlakwas wanya noikniw.	I'm going to eat with my sibling.

Wanya is related to **wan**, which means `and', both to make a list of items and to begin a new sentence.

Nikneki pantsin wan tlaxkalli.	I want bread and tortilla.
Nitlakwas wan nikochis.	I will eat and I will sleep.

Katlinya and **wanya** are both pronounced `katliyya' and `wayya'. They are spelled with the /n/ to show their roots.

In Classical Nahuatl, **Iwan** means `and' when you make a list of items, and **Aw** means `and' when you start a sentence.

Exercise 17 — **How would you say?**

1. Who are you?_____

2. Who is she?_____

3. Who is he?_____

4. Who are they?_____

5. Where are you from?_____

6. Where do you originate?._____

7. How many dogs do you have?_____

8. When is Juan coming?_____

9. What do you eat? _____

10. Why do you dance?_____

11. Why do you learn Nahuatl?_____

12. Why don't you like comedians? _____

tikinpiya	you have (them)	**mihtotia**	to dance
tikinamati	you like (them)	**kamanaloanih**	comedians
momachtia	to study, learn	**tikkwa**	you eat (it)
tiewa	you originate from	**tiwallaw**	you come from
ta	you	**ya**	she/he
wallas	(is) coming	**inihwantin**	they, them

Introductions

Below are some sample phrases that give you some insight as to how to talk about yourself after an introduction. After reading the translations, fill in the blanks with your own information. Locations such as banks, hotels, offices, don't exist in Nahuatl, if needed, fill in with Spanish words.

Nimitstlahpalos! : Greetings/Hello/I greet you!

Na notokah _____ : My name is _____

Na niewa _____ : I originate from _____

Na niwallaw _____ : I come from _____
                       (slight difference in meaning)

Na nikpiya _____ xiwitl : I am _____ years old

Notsonkiska _____ : My last name is _____

Na nikamati _____ : I like to _____

nimihtotis	I dance	**nitekitis**	I work
nitlapowas	I read	**nimomachtis**	I study
nikochis	I sleep	**niyas**	I go to

Na axnikamati _____ : I don't like to _____

Nechpaktia _____: _____ makes me happy

Nitekiti pan _____ : I work at _____.

kaltlamachtiloyan	school	**tepahtiloyan**	hospital, doctor's office
millah	corn fields	**tiankis**	marketplace

Kanin tiyaw? : Where are you going?

Kanin eltok kwatenno? : Where is the bathroom?

Kanin mochan? : Where is your house?

Kanin timokawa? : Where are you staying?

8.

Prepositions

Prepositions tell us the location of actions or nouns in sentences. In Nahuatl, most prepositions are suffixes added onto the end of nouns. However, there are a few prepositions used as standalone words. These prepositions take a possessive pronoun like: no, mo, i.

-wanya / wanya	with (together)	**ika**	with [*no pronoun]
-ixtenno	in front of	**-ika**	behind
-ihtik	inside of	**-kwitlapan**	behind
-nakastlan	next to	**-tsalan**	in between, under
-ixko	in top of	**-pan**	on, over, at

noixtenno - in front of me   **nokwitlapan -** behind me

monakastlan - next to you   **towanya -** with us

In Huasteca Nahuatl, using possessive pronouns on the following words is now optional.

tlan/itlan	if/if X	**pampa/ipampa**	because/ because of it
wanya/iwanya	together/ together with it	**wan/iwan**	and/with it
wahka/iwahka	far/far from it	**nechka/inechka**	close/ close to it

Nikochis tlan nitlakwas. I will sleep if I eat.

Nikochis itlan nitlakwas. I will sleep if I eat.

Nikochmiki mopampa. I'm sleepy because of you.

Nikochmiki pampa ta. I'm sleepy because of you.

Xiwallaw nowanya. Come with me.

Xiwallaw wanya na. Come with me.

Nikneki se chichi iwan se miston. I want a dog and a cat.

Nikneki se chichi wan se miston. I want a dog and a cat.

The first type of prepositions we learned about tell the relationship between people and location (next to me, with me, in front of you). The following prepositions are used exclusively with places, such as: forest, river, store.

There are many prepositional suffixes is Nahuatl, and though many have roughly the same meaning, they are not interchangeable, as a word will typically stick with one type of ending. This means you will simply have to memorize most words as a whole, but knowing the suffix will be useful in breaking down the word into parts. Some of these endings are ancient and no longer used actively, but are preserved or fossilized into certain words. The most common prepositional suffixes are below. Note that -**ko** becomes -**no** when next to an /n/, and -**tlan** becomes -**lan** when next to an /l/.

-k	on over	-ko/-no	on, over
-pan	on, over, at	-tlan/lan	place of

tiankis - market; **tiankisko** - at the market

tlaxkalli - tortilla; **Tlaxkallan** - Tlaxcala (state)

teotl/tiotl - divinity; **tiopan** - church, temple, sacred place

ekatepetl - hill of the wind; **Ekatepek** - at the hill of the wind

Here is a more exhaustive list of prepositional suffixes. While it is not necessary to memorize them all, it can serve as a useful resource when deciphering the names of towns, ranches and cities in Mexico.

-chi	on the floor	**-kan**	place of
-man	place of	**-nawak**	close to
-nalko	opposite side of	**-nepantlah**	in the middle of
-pa	times	**-pal**	with the help of
-pampa	toward	**-pampa**	because of
-techkopa	having to do with	**-tech**	up against
-tlah	abundance of	**-tepotsko**	behind
-titlan	below	**-tlok**	close to
-tsalan	in the middle of	**-tsintlan**	at the base of
-tikpak	on top of	**-yan**	place or time of

Prepositions and Body Parts

Many prepositional words we saw originate from body part words, especially prepositions that relate a person to a location. See the connections:

nonakas	my ear	**nonakastlan**	next to me (place of my ears)
ix-	root that means `face'	**ten-**	root that means -lip, edge
notenxipal	my lips	**noixtenno**	in front of me (place of the face of my lips).
kwitlatl	poop, excrement	**nokwitlapan**	behind me (place of my excrement).
tsin-	root that means `butt, base'	**notsintlan**	at my bottom
notsintamal	my butt		
noikxi	my foot	**noikxitlan**	area by my feet
tson-	root that means `head'	**notsonkiska**	my last name

These prepositions work not only to tell the location relative to humans, but also to people and objects.

tepeixko - at the top of the hill

tepetsintlan - at the base of the hill

tepeikxitlan - at the foot of the hill

One could get detailed in body part vocabulary, including words for intestines, cartilage, etc. We'll focus on the major, most common body part words. Included are previously covered face parts. Body part words must always be possessed. You typically can't just say 'head'.

notsontekon	my head	**notsonkal**	my hair
noikxi	my feet, lower legs	**nomah**	my hands
nomahpil	my fingers	**noihti**	my stomach
noixtiyol	my eyes	**noyakatsol**	my nose
nonakas	my ears	**nokamak**	my mouth
notlankoch	my teeth	**nonenepil**	my tongue
noahkol	my shoulders	**nomets**	my upper legs
noikxopil	my toe	**noomiyo**	my bones
noesso	my blood	**noyollo**	my heart

Practice stating all these body parts. Note that (4) and (11) use the same word in Nahuatl.

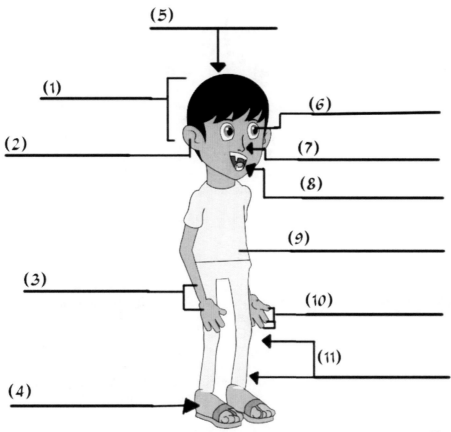

Body parts

Across
2. my tongue
4. his bone
6. your hand

Down
1. your fingers
2. my teeth
3. my stomach
4. his blood
5. his upper legs (thighs)

Regarding private parts: the male body part is **tepolli**, but can also be referred to as **tototl** `bird', and **wilotl** `pigeon'. A myth that **awakatl** comes from male private parts is false, though the reverse can be true, that is, one could say **awakatl** to refer to male private parts. The female private parts are known as **xillan**, which means `womb' in Classical Nahuatl. Female breasts are **chichitl**, not to be confused with `dog'.

Exercise 18 — These are real place names in Mexico, using the word bank below, and the preposition roots previously mentioned, figure out their meanings.

1. Jalisco (Xalixko)

2. Zapotlan (Tzapotlan)

3. Michoacan (Michwahkan)

4. Oaxaca (Waxyakak)

5. Chiapas (Chiapan)

6. Guatemala (Cuauhtemallan)

7. Chicontepec (Chikometepek)

8. Cuernavaca (Kwawnawak)

9. Tula (Tollan)

10. Chapultepec (Chapoltepek)

11. Ajuchitlan (Axochitlan)

a-	water, watery	**xochitl**	flower
tzapotl	sapote fruit	**michwah**	owner of fish
waxin	guaje pod tree	**yakatl**	root meaning `nose '
chian	chia seeds	**chikome**	seven
kwawtli	eagle	**tolli**	rush, tule, cattails
chapollin	grasshopper	**xalli**	sand
kwawtemalli	woodpile, wood filled	**kwawitl**	tree

The origin of the word `Mexico' [**Meexihko**] is a bit of a mystery, though that won't stop many from making big claims. The ending is clearly -ko, but this leaves us with **meexi'**. Some have claimed this to mean **mets-tli** `moon', but -ts- to -x- is not a Nahuatl sound change. Others claimed it to be **metl** + **xiiktli** + **ko** (belly button of maguey plant). However, **metl** has a short /e/, and **Meexihko** has a long /e/. **Xiiktli** has a long /i/ vowel, while **Meexihko** has short /i/, so these also do not match. Finally, there is some possibility it refers to **Mexi**, an ancient ruler of the Mexikah. Other indigenous languages may give us clues. In the Mixteco language, Mexico is called **Ñuu Ko'yo**, but this originally referred to the Toltec empire. In Mezquital Otomi, the word is '**Monda**, which refers to cacti.

9.

How do you feel?

Expressing feelings in Nahuatl is done using verbs. Be careful not to apply the English or Spanish style of stating feelings. For example, English may say I+am+sick, while Nahuatl would structure this as I+sick.

Nimokokoa.   I am sick.

The verb `itstok' should not be used, as it does not mean `I am', but means `I am present'.

Not *Niitstok mokokoa.

Not *Niitstok nimokokoa.

The exception to this is in the question, `How are you?' and the response `I'm good'.

Keniwki tiitstok? How are you?

Tlen kihtoa moyollo? What does your heart say?

Niitstok kwalli.   I am good.

Nochi kwalli. Everything's good.

Nimokokoa	I'm sick	**Nimahmawi**	I'm scared
Nimotekipachoa	I'm worried, burdened	**Nikokoxkati**	I feel weak
Nimayana	I'm hungry	**Nisesekwi**	I'm cold
Nikaxani	I'm healing	**Nikwesiwi**	I'm bored

Many feeling words end in **-tok**. This morpheme (piece of a word) can mean something is in a `state of being', and it's also used on verbs. **Tok** is a type of tense, which means you can't use another tense on top of it, for example, the future **-s** is incompatible with **-tok**. We'll cover **-tok** more coming sections.

Yolpaktok	She's happy	**Siawtok**	He's tired
Mokwesohtok	She's sad	**Yolkwesiwtok**	He's sad
Kwalantok	She's upset	**Mosewihtok**	He's in a state of sitting

Many feeling words end in -**miki** (to die), especially pain related words.

Nikochmiki	I'm sleepy (I'm dying of sleep)	**Niamiki**	I'm thirsty (I'm drying of water)
Nipatsmiki	I'm hot and sweaty (I'm dying of sweat)	**Niapismiki**	I'm hungry (I'm dying of starvation)
Nitlatskamiki	I'm lazy (dying of lazyness)	**Nisokimiki**	I can't stand being dirty (dying from mud)
Nimaxixmiki	I need to pee (dying of pee)	**Nimoxixmiki**	I need to defecate (dying from poop).

Some feeling words begin with the prefix -**nech**-. This hasn't been covered yet, but suffice it to say it means `an action happens to me'.

Nechkokoa notsontekon	My head hurts (me)	**Nechkokoa noihti**	My stomach hurts (me)
Nechtekipachoa	It worries me	**Nechyolkokoa**	He hurts my feelings
Nechpaktia	It pleases me, I like it.		

Stating your opinion can be done with the words: **nikihtoa** `I say, I think that...', **niktlalia** `I place, I think that...', **nimoillia** `I tell myself, I think that...', **nikmachilia** `I feel that'.

> **Nikihtoa ma tiyakan** - I think (say) we should go.

> **Niktlalia ma tiyakan** - I think (put) we should go.

The verb for `to feel' is **machilia**. The section on Transitive verbs with further explain the difference:

> **Nimomachilia kenwak nimokokoa**- I feel like I'm sick.

> **Nikmachilia nimokokoa** - I think that I'm sick.

You may have noticed the similarities between **nimaxixmiki** and **nimoxixmiki**. The root -**xixa**- means `to poop, defecate', while the addition of **atl** `water' in **axixa**, changes the defecation to a watery substance, i.e. pee. These are more examples of adding pieces to build words in Nahuatl. The use of a- is very common, and can imply `water, liquid' or `watery'.

Conversation

Lupeh: Piyali Lenoh. Keniwki tiitstok?

Lenoh: Axkwalli niitstok noikniw.

Lupeh:Axkwalli timomachilia?

Lenoh: Kena.

Lupeh: Wan nopa kenke?

Lenoh: Nimokokoa.

Lupeh: Keniwki?

Lenoh: Nechkokoa notsontekon.

Lupeh: Nikihtoa xikochi wan xikoni achiyok atl.

Lenoh: Melawak?

Lupeh: Kena. Wan niwallas tlan nokka timokokoa.

Lenoh: Tlaskamati.

Lupeh: Axtlen. Nimotekipachoa tlan timokokoa.

oni	to drink something	**achiyok**	more, a little more
atl	water	**melawak**	really, truthfully
nokka	still	**tlaskamati**	thank you
axtlen	it's nothing	**tlan**	if
tekipachoa	to worry (nimo)		

Tlaskamati is the Huasteca equivalent of **tlasohkamati** in central varieties. **Tlasoh** is not an acceptable simplification.

Vocabulary: Sickness

To continue this section's theme, below are more words which can be used to state one's feelings. Note that there aren't many specific words for types of viruses. These specific words, when needed, are typically borrowed from Spanish. It's more common for the symptoms to be talked about and dealt with.

Some words here begin with /m/ or /mo/, they imply a reflexive action, in that you are doing something to yourself, consciously or not.

mokokoa	to be sick	**mihsotla**	to throw up
mokechtsaktok	to be hoarse	**mihyexa**	to pass gas
mihtsomia	to blow one's nose	**mitonia**	to sweat
		melpotsa	to burp

tsikwinoa	to have hiccups	**tlatlasi**	to cough
yakatsonpiliwi	to have a runny nose	**yakaatemo**	to have a runny nose
totoniya	to have a fever	**kokolistli**	a sickness
sawatl	smallpox, rash	**kokotl**	sores, pimple
ahwayowa	to be itchy	**temi**	to fill up, get swollen
ahkwexoa	to sneeze	**tlanokia**	to have diarrhea
tlapoloa	to faint		

kokolistli

Across

6. I cough
8. You are itchy

Down

1. You sweat
2. I have a fever
3. You faint
4. I throw up
5. You have diarrhea
7. I'm sick

Intensifiers: Tlawel, Miak

One more way create new sentences with feeling vocabulary would be to add intensifiers. **Tlawel** and **miak** are the main intensifiers in Nahuatl, but they can be a cause for confusion. To put it simply, **tlawel** intensifies an action, a verb, or adjective, and is more of a true intensifier. **Miak**, by contrast, translates best to `many' or `a lot' (but not `a lot' as an intensifier). These words tend to go before the word it modifies.

tlawel	very, much, a lot	**miak**	many, a lot

Tlawel nikochmiki. - I'm very sleepy.

Tlawel nitekiti. - I work a lot (intensely).

Tlawel weyi ni kaltlamachtiloyan.- This school is very big.

Tlaskamati miak - Many thanks

Tlawel tlaskamati - Thank a lot (intensely)

Nikneki miak tlaxkalli - I want <u>many</u> tortillas

Tlawel nikneki tlaxkalli - I very much <u>want</u> tortillas

To do the opposite of intensifying, you can use the words **kentsin** (a little, or a tiny amount), and **achi/achitsin** (a small amount). **Kentsin** can be used both for intensity and quantity, but **achitsin** is typically used only for quantity.

Nikneki san achi tlaxkalli - I just want few tortillas.

Nikneki san kentsin tlaxkalli - I just want very little tortillas.

Kentsin nikochmiki. - I'm a little sleepy.

In central varieties, **tlawel** becomes **wel**, and **miak** can be **miek**. Instead of **kentsin**, you may hear **tepitsin**.

10.

Transitive Verbs

Understanding transitive verbs is one of the biggest breakthroughs required for any student to gain fluency in Nahuatl. Nearly every action word makes a distinction between transitive and intransitive verbs, and with this new skill, you will be able to break down most verbs in Nahuatl.

To put it simply, Nahuatl makes a distinction between verbs that are *simple/intransitive*, and verbs that are *transitive*. Transitive verbs are those that do an action to someone or an object like: hit, give, sell. Simple sentences don't have an object, and include verbs like: walk, run sleep. The distinction is clearer to see when they are compared side by side.

Intransitive	Transitive
John <u>runs.</u>	John <u>kicked the ball.</u>
Marcos <u>walks.</u>	Marcos <u>walks his dog.</u>
Julia <u>danced.</u>	Julia <u>danced the dog</u> (made it dance).
I <u>woke up.</u>	Miguel <u>woke me up.</u>
He <u>slept.</u>	The medicine <u>put him to sleep.</u>

The important takeaway here is that transitive verbs <u>need</u> to have an object, while intransitives <u>cannot</u> have an object. Consider how awkward this can sound even in English.

Intransitive	Transitive
*I laughed the car.	*John kicked.
*He cried the boy.	*The medicine put to sleep.

A word that is transitive/intransitive in English may not be the same in Nahuatl. A proper Nahuatl dictionary should tell the reader whether a verb is intransitive by labeling the verb as (**ni**), while a transitive verb should be labelled with (**nik**). Let's find out why.

Recall this chart for verbs in present tense. This chart is for **intransitive verbs**. There is no room or space for objects. It only has space for the **subject**, the one doing the action.

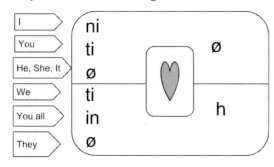

Nitlakwa - I eat
Titlakwa - You eat
Tlakwa - She eats
Titlakwah - We eat
Intlakwah - Ya'll eat
Tlakwah - They eat

Now we have below a chart for transitive verbs. Note how it requires both the subject and the object. There are several objects, but for now, we'll focus only on the object /**k**/. Here **-ihtoa** is a transitive verb that means (to say something), so it requires both a subject, and an object, in this case, /**k**/.

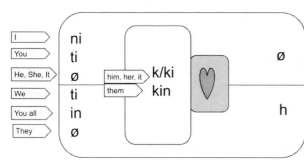

Nikihtoa - I say it
Tikihtoa - You say it
Kihtoa - He says it
Tikihtoah - We say it
Inkihtoah - Ya'll say it
Kihtoah - They say it

In this case, we couldn't use the object **-kin-**, because it means `to them'. If we used it, we would be saying **nikinihtoa** `I say them', which makes no sense. Let's see a full paradigm that demonstrates both.

Nikitta - I see it   **Nikinitta** - I see them
Tikitta - You see it   **Tikinitta** - You see them
Kiitta - He sees it   **Kinitta** - He sees them
Tikittah - We see it   **Tikinittah** - We see them
Inkittah - Ya'll see it   **Inkinittah** - Ya'll see them
Kittah - They see it   **Kinittah** - They see them

Now you can better understand some patterns we've seen before.

Nikihtoa ya nikochis. - I think I'll sleep now.

Nikneki nitlakwas. - I want to eat.

Juan kineki kochis - Juan wants to sleep.

Nikamati chokolatl. - I like chocolate.

Nikitta se tototl kakaahko. - I see a bird up there.

We can apply transitive verbs with the future tense as well.

Nikihtos. - I will say it.

Tikihtos. - You will say it.

Tikihtoseh. - We will say it.

We can also apply transitive verbs with commands.

Xikihto! - Say it!

Xikihtokan! - You all say it!

Xikchiwa - Do it!

Ma tikchiwakan - Let's do it.

Pronunciation of /k/

When /k/ is at the end of a syllable, it may sound like a soft /h/ sound. You will likely see Nahuatl speakers spell both ways, depending if they are being strict with writing how it sounds, or strict with writing the underlying, root sound.

Writing the origin	Writing the changed sound
nikneki	nihneki (or) nijneki
xikchiwa	xihchiwa (or) xijchiwa
tikneki	tihneki (or) tijneki
nikchiwas	nihchiwas (or) nijchiwas

Vocabulary: Transitives

amati	to like something/someone	**neki**	to want something/someone
kawa	to leave something/someone	**chiwa**	to do something
chiya	to wait for someone	**kowa**	to buy something
mati	to know, sense something	**piya**	to have something
tsakwa	to close something	**tlapoa**	to open something
ihkwiloa	to write something	**powa**	to read something

Transitives

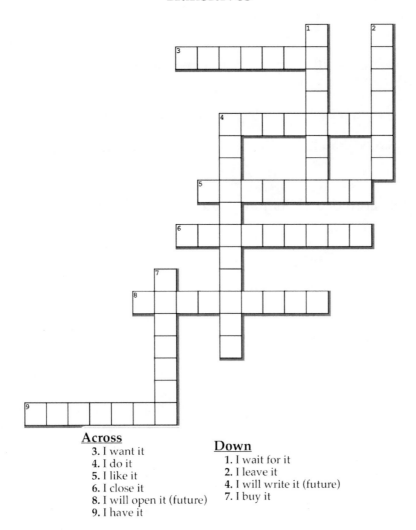

Across
3. I want it
4. I do it
5. I like it
6. I close it
8. I will open it (future)
9. I have it

Down
1. I wait for it
2. I leave it
4. I will write it (future)
7. I buy it

So far in this chapter we've learned that there are two basic types of verbs in Nahuatl: transitive and intransitive. Intransitive verbs can only take a subject, and transitives require both a subject and object. In other words, a transitive verb must always be satisfied with some type of object prefix. We'll remember this principle again in the future when we learn to convert verbs to nouns, where once again we'll need to satisfy the transitive verb's object with special considerations.

Can you figure out what errors were produced here?

1. *Niitta. -I see it.

2. *Nineki. - I want it.

3. *Juan neki etlakwalli. - Juan wants a bean meal.

In all these cases, the transitive verb was not satisfied with an object, thus creating sentences that make no sense in Nahuatl.

Checking dictionaries will help you know the difference between similar sounding words like these:

Nikwika - I take it (from **wika `transitive'**)

Niwika - I sing (from **wika `intransitive**)

Exercise 19.   Here is a list of verbs. Figure out whether it's transitive or intransitive based on the definition and example.

Word	Definition	Transitive or Intransitive?
saniloa	to talk (nisaniloa)	
sanilwia	to talk to someone (niksanilwia)	
kwa	to eat something (nikkwa)	
wallaw	to come (niwallaw)	
tlakwa	to eat (nitlakwa)	
tlatla	for something to burn (tlatla)	
tlatia	to burn something, turn something on (niktlatia)	
tlehko	to climb up (nitlehko)	
toka	to plant something, to bury something (niktoka)	
toka	to plant seeds (nitoka)	

To Say, Tell, Talk

A common error for beginners is the confusion between **ihtoa** and **illia/ilwia** (**illia** and **ilwia** are synonyms). They both mean `to say', and they both are transitive. The general distinction, however, is that **ihtoa** means `to say something', focusing on the words, while **illia** means `to tell someone something', focusing on telling a person.

**Nikihtoa `tlaskamati' ipan noaltepew.** - I say `tlaskamati' in my town.

Nikillia Juan `tlaskamati' pampa kichiwa kwalli. - I say thanks to because he does good.

Finally, there are many words that mean `to talk'. They are synonyms, most understood by all towns in the Huasteca.

Intransitive

kamati	to talk (to use your mouth)	saniloa	to talk (comes from **sanilli**, to tell riddles, jokes)
nawati	to speak Nahuatl	tlahtoa	to speak; to speak Spanish. (see how it's related to **ihtoa**).

Transitive

kamawia	to converse with someone	sanilwia	to talk with someone
illia/ilwia	to tell someone (something)	ihtoa	to say (something)

Other Regions

Guerrero and Central regions only understand the word **tlahtoa**. Other regions employ the word **tlapowi** `to talk'.

Speaking a language

The verb **saniloa** tends to be used with the word **ika** (with) when talking about speaking languages.

Nisaniloa ika Nawatl. I Speak Nahuatl.

One last point about transitives is to remember that the third person singular subject (he/she) exists without any sound. We represent this subject with ∅.

Kiitta (He sees her).
∅-ki-itta   (∅=He; ki = her; itta = see)

When we have a ∅ followed by a /k/, the /k/ is left in the front of the word. If the verb begins with a vowel, this causes us to have two possible pronunciations of the word, one with /k/ and one with /ki/. Both are acceptable.

He sees it (itta)	**Kiitta**	**Kitta**
He says it (ihtoa)	**Kiihtoa**	**Kihtoa**
She likes him (amati)	**Kiamati**	**Kamati**

Huasteca Nahuatl lets you keep both vowels when they meet, but Central varieties require you to merge both vowels, thus only producing the set on the right.

Exercise 20 — Tlen kihtosneki?

1. Nikihtoa _____

2. Tikihtoa_____

3. Tikihtoah _____

4. Inkihtoah _____

5. Nikihtos _____

6. Tikihtoseh _____

7. Inkisewiah _____

8. Tiksewiah _____

9. Kisewiseh _____

10. Nikneki _____

11. Niknekis _____

12. Nikchiwas _____

13. Nikamati nimihtotis _____

14. Nikamati niwikas _____

15. tikamatih tiwikaseh. _____

amati	to like something/ one	**sewia**	to turn something off, cool something off
chiwa	to do something	**ihtoa**	to say something
mihtotia	to dance	**wika**	to sing
neki	to want/love something/ someone.		

Exercise 21 — Keniwki moillia?

1. I like him/her _____

2. You like him/her_____

3. He likes her _____

4. She likes him _____

5. We like her _____

6. They like him _____

7. I want it _____

8. You love him _____

9. You do it_____

10. They do it_____

11. You all do it_____

12. I do it_____

13. I turn it off_____

11.

Possession II

Let's briefly return to the concept of possessing nouns. We previously learned the possessive pronouns to be:

No- `my'          **Mo-**     `your'   **I-** `his/her'

To- `our'          **Inmo-**   `ya'lls'   **Inin-** `their'

This allowed us to create simply sentences such as **nochichi, mochichi, ichichi, tochichi** etc., as well as plural possessed nouns **nochichiwan, mochichiwan, tochichiwan, inmochichiwan, ininchichiwan** etc.

All of these words thus far are actually just the third person subject pronouns (he, she, they).

nowelti-w   **noweltiwan**
Ø-no-welti-w   Ø-no-welti-wan
my sister/She <u>is</u> my sister.   my sisters/<u>They are</u> my sisters.

What we want to learn to say now is `<u>I am</u> your sister', `<u>You are</u> my sister', `<u>We are</u> your sisters', etc. See the examples below, where **awi** means `aunt'.

	no-	mo-	i-	to-	inmo-	inin-
ni-	-----	nimoawi	niiawi	------	niinmoawi	niininawi
ti-	tinoawi	------	tiiawi	titoawi	-----	tiininawi
Ø-	noawi	moawi	iawi	toawi	inmoawi	ininawi
ti-	------	timoawiwan	tiiawiwan	----	tiinmoawiwan	tiininawian
in-	innoawiwan	-----	iniawiwan	intoawiwan	-----	inininawiwan
Ø-	noawiwan	moawiwan	iawiwan	toawiwan	inmoawiwan	ininawiwan

Some of the combinations are left blank because they would not generally make sense (i.e. You are the brother of you all).

Here's some translations, try to read the rest.

Nimoawi. I am your aunt.

Niiawi. I am her aunt.

Niinmoawi. I am the aunt of ya'll.

This chart gives us a second look at how the complete possessives are structured. The first set are the subjects, followed by who possesses them. Note the ending -wan is blocked from the possessive pronouns. This is because they have nothing to do with each other. -Wan is used when you have plural subjects only (ti, in, Ø), its not tied to the plural pronouns (to, inmo, inin).

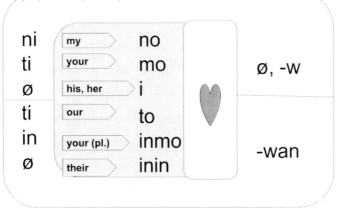

Tochichi. <u>It's</u> our do<u>g</u>.

Tochichiwan. <u>They're</u> our dog<u>s</u>.

> Plural nouns use -meh in any other instance except when possessed. Here, plural nouns use -wan. Careful not to confuse the two.

TE: Someone's

Certain nouns need to always be possessed. This is especially common in family and body part words. So if want to say `mother' without referring to who she has that relationship with, we can say `someone's mother'. The prefix that handles this in Nahuatl is `Te-', which means the object belongs to someone, without mention who.

techan - someone's home

tenantsin - someone's mother; madam; middle-aged woman

tetahtsin - someone's father; man, sir; middle-aged man

teikniw - someone's sibling

Exercise 22 — Tlen Kihtosneki?

1. Tinotatah_____

2. Tinonanan_____

3. Nonanan _____

4. Totatah _____

5. Noichpokaw _____

6. Toichpokaw _____

7. Toichpokawan _____

8. Notatahwan _____

9. Itelpokaw_____

10. Itelpokawan_____

11. Ininmachikniwan_____

12. Tokonewan_____

13. Inmokonewan_____

14. Nototatah _____

15. Nototatahwan _____

16. Tiikonew Maria? _____

Check the word bank for irregularities. Some nouns appear different when possessed. Also note that `father' when plural, implies `parents'

Exercise 23 — Keniwki moillia?

1. You are my sister_____

2. Is she your sister?_____

3. He is your young man _____

4. They are your young girls _____

5. He is your little boy _____

6. She is your little girl _____

7. It's our land _____

8. Is she your student? _____

9. Is she your teacher?_____

10. They are my teachers_____

11. He is my grandfather_____

12. They are my grandparents_____

13. Ya'll are my children_____

14. Are you Maria's child? _____

15. Are you Juan's father? _____

16. Luke, I am your father _____

tlalli	land	**momachtihketl**	student
tlalwi	land (when possessed)	**momachtihka**	student (when possessed)
tepostli	metal	**tlamachtihketl**	teacher
weltiw	sister	**tlamachtihka**	teacher (when possessed)
siwapil	little girl	**iknitl**	sibling
okichpil	little boy	**ichpokatl**	teenage girl
machiknitl	cousin	**telpokatl**	teenage boy
tatah	father	**-tatahwan**	parents
totatah	grandfather	**-totatahwan**	grandparents

Vocabulary: Family

Family words are generally always possessed. It's generally not grammatically correct to say **iknitl** 'sibling', by itself, for example. Below are more family kin terms.

Noteixmatkawan
My family members

nochocho
'my younger sibling'
(Huasteca only)

nomimi
'my older brother'
(Huasteca only)

nopipi
'my older sister'
(Huasteca only)

noweltiw
'my sister'

nonanan
'my mother'

notatah
'my father'

nototatah
'my grandfather'

notonanan
'my grandmother'

noikniw
'my sibling'

notlayi
'my uncle'

noawi
'my aunt'

nokonew
'my child'

nosiwaw
'my wife/woman'

notlakaw
'my husband/man'

noweweh
'my old husband'

noixwiw
'my grandchild'

Family members related to your parents are marked with **mach**.

nomachikniw
'my cousin'

nomachkonew
'my niece/
nephew'

These words, when possessed, imply one's child of the corresponding age.

ichpokatl
'teenage daughter'

telpokatl
'teenage son'

siwapil
'young girl'

okichpil
'young boy'

Outside of the Huasteca, these words are used to refer to grandparents.

noweyitatah
'my grandpa'

noweyinanan
'my grandma

nokoltsin
'my ancient, grandpa'

nosihtsin
'my ancient, grandma'

Most In-laws have a specialized vocabulary dealing with whether the speaker is male or female. Note the patterns of -**yex**-, -**mon**- -**weh**.

Females only	Males only
noyexnan `my mother-in-law'	**nomonnan** `my mother-in-law'
noyextah `my father-in-law'	**nomontah** `my father-in-law'
nowehpol `my brother-in-law'	**nowehpol** `my sister-in-law'
nowes `my sister-in-law'	**notex** `my brother-in-law'
noyeyohtikapoh `my brother-in-law's wife'	**nomontikapoh** `my sister-in-law's husband'

These in-law words apply to both male and female.

noyeyohwi
`my daughter-in-law'

nomontli
`my son-in-law'
(note this unique noun doesn't
drop the -tli)

Step siblings have a common morpheme of -**tepots**-.

notepotskonew
`my stepchild'

notepotsikniw
`my step sibling'

notepotsnanan
`my step mother'

notepotstatah
`my step father'

notepotsmachikniw
`my step cousin'

Other related vocabulary:

towahkapawan
`our ancestors' (people from
long ago)

iknotsin
`orphan'

ilamatsin
`elder lady, or slang for child
who sits on the floor like an
old lady'

wewetsin
`general term for old person'

Nahuatl Baptisms: Notokayoh

Mexican Spanish retains an ancient Nahuatl word `tocayo', generally used to refer to someone with your same name. **Notoka** is from Nahuatl meaning `my name', while the **-yo** here implies `fellow, person like me, namesake'. We see this in only a few possessed nouns.

<table>
<tr><td>

nowampoh
`my friend'
</td><td>

nowampoyowan
`my friends'
</td></tr>
<tr><td>

notekixpoh
`my friend, coworker'
</td><td>

notekixpoyowan
`my friends, coworkers'
</td></tr>
<tr><td>

notokah
`my name'
</td><td>

notokayo
`my fellow namesake'
</td></tr>
</table>

The use of **tokayo** can be found in Nahuatl baptism ceremony practices. Godmothers and their Goddaughters will call each other by the same name, thus connection a relationship between each other through the name. Likewise, Godfathers and Godsons will do the same. Across gender lines, participants will call each other as if they were spouses.

	To Godmother	To Godfather	To Goddaughter	To Godson
Godmother	----	----	notokah	noweweh
Godfather	----	----	nosiwaw	notokayo
Goddaughter	notokah	noweweh	----	----
Godson	nosiwaw	notokayo	----	----

Irregular Possession

Few nouns take an ancient form **-wi** when possessed. Most were changed to -w, which were then changed to an -h sound. Here are the most common.

<table>
<tr><td>

pahtli
`medicine'
</td><td>

nopahwi
`my medicine'
</td></tr>
<tr><td>

ohtli
`road'
</td><td>

noohwi
`my road'
</td></tr>
<tr><td>

tlalli
`land'
</td><td>

notlalwi
'my land'
</td></tr>
</table>

Inalienable Possession

Nahuatl, like many Uto-Aztecan languages, makes use of a property called `Inalienable Possession'. This refers to groups of nouns that are required to be possessed, they cannot be alienated or removed and they inherently belong to its possessor. We've seen this briefly with family terms and body parts. However, there are forms for certain body parts that do not necessarily belong to a person. For example, one could a bone on the floor, and it may not belong to a human at all.

In these cases, Nahuatl can make a distinction between a noun, and an inalienable noun, by having the inalienable noun carry the ending -yo. This may be a different -yo from `fellow, namesake' which we just explored. Note that -yo can change sounds through influence from nearby sounds. See the examples below.

omitl `a general bone'	**noomiyo** `my bone'
estli `blood, in general'	**noesso** `my blood'
xochitl `a flower in general'	**-xochiyo** `a plants flower'
xiwitl `a plant, herb'	**-xiwiyo** `a plant's leaves'
nakatl `meat'	**nonakayo** `my body'

Both sets of nouns can be possessed should it be necessary. Saying **nonaka**, for example, would imply you are possessing meat which you are going to eat. **Nonakayo**, on the other hand, would only be used to refer to your own meat, i.e. your body.

Agentives

The term agentives refers to nouns that describe people, often taken from verbs. In English, the most common agentive is -er (teacher, worker, dancer, writer etc). Nahuatl makes use of two agentive endings, one for singular (**ketl**) and one for plural (-**nih**).

-**ketl**	-**nih**
tekitiketl	**tekitinih**
`worker'	`workers'
iwintiketl	**iwintinih**
`drunk person'	`several drunk people'

When using -**ketl**, you will have to remove the -**a** in words that end in -**ia/oa**. An -**h**- takes the place of the -**a**-.

motlalohketl	**motlaloanih**
`runner'	`runners'
momachtihketl	**momachtianih**
'student'	`students'
tlamachtihketl	**tlamachtianih**
`teacher'	`teachers'

Several other verbs will lose the final vowel when using -**ketl**. These belong to a group called `class 2' verbs, which will be further covered in an upcoming chapter.

tlaichtekketl	**tlaichtekinih**
`robber'	`robbers'
tlayekanketl	**tlayekananih**
`leader'	`leaders'

Because these words lost their vowel, the combination of two consonants next to each other can cause sounds to change. Most notably, /kk/ will become /hk/, and /yk/ will become /xk/.

kwatlakketl	(no plural)
`thing which fruited, a fruit'	
tlachixketl	**tlachiyanih**
`observer, type of shaman'	`observers, type of shaman'

A unique change occurs with the word **mikketl** (dead person). This word is considered rude by itself, so it takes the form **mikkatsin**, taking the -**tsin** form for politeness. This means the plural form would be **mikkatsitsin**.

In Central varieties, the most common agentives use -**ni** for the singular, and -**nimeh** for the plural, with no dropping of vowels.

temachtiani 'teacher'	**temachtianimeh** `teachers'
tlawanani `drunk person'	**tlawananimeh** `drunk people'

Lastly, we can possess agentives, which also have a unique rule. All sound change rules remain the same as with -**ketl**. Any ia/oa endings change the /a/ into an /h/. Then, one adds -**kaw** for the singular, and -**kawan** for the plural.

notekitikaw `'my worker'	**notekitikawan** `my workers'
nomomachtihkaw `my student'	**nomomachtihkawan** `my students'
notlamachtihkaw `my teacher'	**notlamachtihkawan** `my teachers'
notlayekankaw `my leader'	**notlayekankawan** `my leaders'

Exercise 24 — Keniwki moillia?

1. You are my student_____

2. You are my teacher_____

3. I am your student_____

4. I am your teacher _____

5. You all are my teachers _____

Te- and Tla-

Before taking any verb and forming an agentive construction from it, we have to consider whether the verb is intransitive or transitive. An intransitive verb needs no modification, it can automatically take -**ketl** or -**nih** just with the sound changes we've seen. The following are intransitive.

nehnemi (to walk)	**nehnenketl** (a walker)
choka (to cry)	**chokaketl** (a crier, crybaby)
tlatsiwi (to be lazy)	**tlatsiwketl** (a lazy person)
tekiti (to work)	**tekitiketl** (a worker)

Transitive verbs, however, cannot be used by themselves or they would make no sense. Remember: Transitive verbs need to be `satisfied' with some form of an object marker; but the object prefixes (nech, mits, ki, tech, mech, kin) would make no sense. Instead, we have two special prefixes: **te-** and **tla-**. **Te-** implies an unspecified person, and **tla-** implies an unspecified object.

-machtia to teach someone	> **temachtia** > he teaches someone	> **temachtihketl** > a teacher of people
-machtia to teach someone	> **tlamachtia** > he teaches things	> **tlamachtihketl** > a teacher of things
-ihkwiloa to write s.t.	> **tlahkwiloa** > to write stuff	> **tlahkwilohketl** > a writer
-motla to shoot s.t.	> **tlamotla** > he shoots things	> **tlamotlaketl** > a shooter
-miktia to kill someone	> **temiktia** > he kills people	> **temiktihketl** > a killer

This next example contains an error, how could you fix it?

-palewia to help someone	> **palewia** > he helps	> **palewihketl** > a helper

Exercise 25 — Try to create these agentive words. Remember to first consider whether a word is transitive or intransitive.

1. A giver (to people)_____

2. A giver (of things) _____

3. A seller (of things)._____

4. A receiver (of stuff)_____

5. A dancer_____

6. A believer (of stuff) _____

7. A visitor (of people) _____

8. A drunkard_____

9. A shouter_____

namaka	to sell something	**maka**	to give something to someone
selia	to receive something	**mihtotia**	to dance
neltoka	to believe something	**paxaloa**	to visit someone
iwinti	to get drunk	**tsahtsi**	to shout

One last point about transitive verbs is that they can be satisfied by taking nouns directly fused onto the verb.

-namaka	**xochinamaka**	**xochinamakaketl**
to sell something	he sells flowers	a flower vendor

-saka	**asaka**	**asakaketl**
to transport s.t.	he transports water	water transporter

12.

Transitive Verbs II

In this chapter, we will complete the paradigm for transitive verbs. Previously, we learned about the 3rd person object prefix (**k/ki**) as well as (**kin**). To complete the rest of the prefixes, we need to learn how to express actions done (to me), (to us), (to you), (to you all).

nech- (to me)	**mits-** (to you)	**k/ki-** (to him, her)
tech- (to us)	**mech-** (to you all)	**kin-** (to them)

Below is the full paradigm with each possibility. Try to break down every example so you can better comprehend the patterns involved. By understanding this structure and knowing just one verb, can you guess how many different words we can produce? One transitive verb can produce about 30 conjugations just in the present tense. Now imagine knowing 40 verbs, that's 1,200 different sentences. The possibilities are endless!

Nimitsitta	I see you	Timitsittah	We see you
Nikitta	I see him/her	Tikittah	We see him/her
Nitechitta	I see us		
Nimechitta	I see you all	Timechittah	We see you all
Nikinitta	I see them	Tikinittah	We see them

Tinechitta	You see me	Innechittah	You all see me
Tikitta	You see him/her	Inkittah	You all see him/her
Titechitta	You see us	Intechittah	You all see us
Tikinitta	You see them	Inkinittah	You all see them

Nechitta	She sees me	Nechittah	They see me
Mitsitta	She sees you	Mitsittah	They see you
Kiitta	She sees him	Kiittah	They see him/her
Techitta	She sees us	Techittah	They see us
Mechitta	She sees you all	Mechittah	They see you all
Kinitta	She sees them	Kinittah	They see them

This chart represents our knowledge of transitive verbs in the present tense.

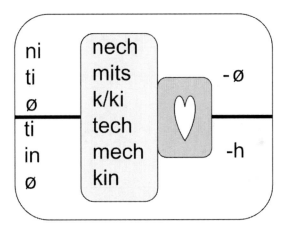

For the future tense, all that changes is the ending, which represents the tense. This same logic will apply to more tenses we will see in coming chapters.

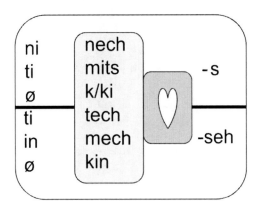

Nimitsittas   I will see you |**Timitsittaseh** We will see you

You may have noticed both /k/ and /ki/ can represent `he, she it', but they are not interchangeable. The prefix /ni-/, /ti-/, and /ti-/ all use /k/. The /ø/ can use either /k/ or /ki/. It uses /k/ if the next sound is a consonant and (may) use /ki/ if the next sound is a vowel. The subject /in/ typically uses /ki/.

(to want) nikneki, tikneki, kineki, tiknekih, inkinekih, kinekih

(to say) nikitta, tikitta, kiitta / kitta, tikittah, inkiittah, kiittah

Exercise 26 — Tlen kihtosneki?

1. Xinechilli._____

2. Xinechchiya._____

3. Nimitschiyas._____

4. Nimitsillia._____

5. Kena nimitskwamachilia._____

6. Naman nikkwamachilia. _____

7. Amo nimechkwamachilia. _____

8. Nimitsneki. _____

9. Tinechneki? _____

10. Xikilli. _____

11. Nimechillis. _____

12. Xinechchiyakan. _____

13. Tikkwamachilia? _____

14. Timitskokoliah. _____

15. Innechkokoliah? _____

Amo nimitskwamachilia, welis yolik xikihto?

I don't understand you, could you say it slowly?

The verb **kwamachilia** 'to understand s.t.' breaks down into **kwa** (a prefix that means *head*) and **machilia** (to feel). Other towns in the Huasteca simply say **machilia** to mean (to understand). Still other regions say **ahsikamati**, which literally means (to reach knowing).

Exercise 27 — Keniwki moillia?

1. I hate it._____

2. I hate you._____

3. I hate them._____

4. You hate me._____

5. You hate him._____

6. You hate them. _____

7. Do you hate us? _____

8. Will you wait for me?_____

9. Will you wait for us?_____

10. Now I understand (it). _____

11. Do they want us? _____

12. They will tell me._____

13. She will tell you today_____

14. He won't wait for you. _____

15. We will wait for you. _____

16. Does he understand it? _____

amati	to like s.t.	**illia**	to say s.t. to s.o.
neki	to love/want s.o.	**chiya**	to wait for s.o.
kokolia	to hate s.o.	**kwamachilia**	to understand s.t. or s.o.
kena	yes	**naman**	now, today

Note: In order to save space, I simplify `someone' to s.o. and `something' to s.t.

Reflexives

One item that was missing from our paradigm was reflexives, or, actions that one does to himself/herself. These combinations are not grammatical.

*Ninechitta. I see myself   ***Timitsitta.** You see yourself

Instead, the reflexives are expressed with the morpheme -mo-. This prefix goes before the verb, but after the subject pronouns. -mo- will generally not be used simultaneously with an object prefix, so one or the other will be used.

Nimoitta. I see myself   **Timoitta**. You see yourself.

Moitta. She sees herself.   **Timoittah**. We see ourselves

Inmoittah. Ya'll see yourselves.   **Moittah**. They see themselves.

-mo- is also used for reciprocal actions, meaning when people do an action to each other. Naturally this only happens with plural subjects. Thus the words can have a second meanings.

Timoittah. We see each other   **Inmoittah**. Ya'll see each other.

Moittah. They see each other.

The third function of -mo- is that it essentially fulfills the role of the passive tense. This means we can say an action is done without indicating *who* did the action.

Monakama tamalli.
Tamales are sold.   **Motekiwia tlikolli**
A pen is used.

Moneki niyas.
It's necessary that I leave.   **Mochiwa.**
It is made.

Beginners often confuse the reflexive **mo-** with the 2nd person singular possessive **mo-** (yours). Keep a look out between them. Consider that the reflexive only goes on verbs, and the possessive only goes on nouns.

In Classical Nahuatl, the reflexive **-mo-** actually had three forms, depending on which subject pronoun was used. **-no-** was only for (my), **-to-** was only for (our), and the rest used **-mo-**. **-mo-** became the default in most modern towns.

Ni<u>no</u>itta	Ti<u>to</u>ittah
Ti<u>mo</u>itta	An<u>mo</u>ittah
<u>Mo</u>itta	<u>Mo</u>ittah

In the modern Guerrero region, **-no-** actually became the default.

Ni<u>no</u>itta	Ti<u>no</u>ittah
Ti<u>no</u>itta	An<u>no</u>ittah
<u>No</u>itta	<u>No</u>ittah

Looking back at verbs we've previously covered, you may have noticed some began with **-mo**. These verbs were actually carrying the reflexive **-mo** all along.

Nimomachtia
I study. (Literally, I teach myself)

Nimokokoa
I'm sick. (Literally, I hurt myself)

Nimotlaloa
I run. (Literally, I run myself. Thus, -run- is transitive here).

Motekiwia se tlikolli.
A pen is used.

Keep in mind that **-mo-** only attaches to transitive verbs. It cannot be used with intransitive verbs. These two examples won't make sense.

*Nimokochi
`I sleep myself'

If you want to imply that you do an action `by yourself', you can use a special ending **-ya**, at the end of the independent pronoun.

nahaya - me myself	**tohwantinya** - us ourselves
tahaya - you yourself	**inmohwantinya** - ya'll yourselves
yahaya - she herself	**inihwantinya** - they themselves

Exercise 28 — Keniwki moillia?

1. It is understood _____

2. It is said _____

3. Maria and I see each other _____

4. I cut myself _____

5. I sit down (I sit myself) _____

6. I tell myself _____

7. We talk to each other _____

sewia   1. To cool something off (nik). 2. To sit down (nimo).

kwamachilia   to understand something

sanilwia   to talk to someone

illia   1. To tell someone s.t. (nik)
2. To think (nimo)

ihtoa   to say s.t.

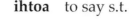

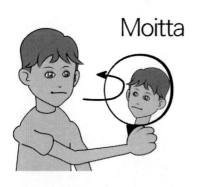

Moitta

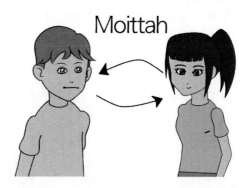

Moittah

Some reflexive nouns may swallow up the /o/ if the verb starts with a vowel. The verb **maltia** `to shower oneself' is actually **altia** `to shower someone' with a reflexive /mo/ attached onto it. The same situation occurs with **mawiltia** `to play', which is actually **awiltia** with the reflexive. In these particular cases, overly emphasizing the reflexive may change the meaning. In the examples below, notice only the verbs starting with vowels can make the obvious change.

Nim<u>ax</u>ixa `I urinate'        Nimo<u>ax</u>ixa `I urinate myself'

Nimo<u>xix</u>a `I defecate'        Nimo<u>xix</u>a `I defecate myself'

Adjectives

Adjectives are words that describe nouns, like `big, pretty, yellow, small'. The word order of Nahuatl is not nearly as strict as English. See how we can move the adjective to come before or after the word it modifies.

> Weyi notekixpoh. - My friend is big.

> Notekixpoh weyi. - My friend is big.

The general description words are below. Note many end in -k, which is related to the past tense.

weyi	big	**kwekwetstsin**	small
echkapantsin	short in height	**wahkapantik**	tall
pitsawak	thin	**patlawak**	wide
tomawak	fat	**wiwi**	dumb, foolish
wehweyak	long	**kototstsin**	short
yankwik	new	**sosoltik**	old (object)
alaxtik	smooth	**yamanik**	soft, warm
yehyektsin	pretty	**fierotik/ axyehyektsin**	ugly

Words that end in **-tsin** are reduplicated to **-tsitsin** for the plural. Adjectives that end in **-k** are pluralized to **-keh**. Adjectives that end in **-tik** are pluralized to **-tikeh**. **Weyi** is pluralized by reduplication.

> **tomawakeh** - obese people (plural)

> **wehweyi** - big things

> **yehyektsitsin** - pretty (plural)

> **wahkapantikeh** - tall people (plural)

The basis for creating new adjectives is most commonly done with the ending -**tik** which attaches to nouns. Take for example the word `water' **atl**. By adding -**tik**, and of course removing the absolutive ending (tl), we can create the adjective **atik**, meaning `something like water, or, watery'.

tetl (rock)	**tetik** (strong)
etl (beans)	**etik** (heavy)
atolli (gruel)	**atoltik** (a liquid thick like gruel)
chilli (chili pepper)	**chichiltik** (the color red)
teskatl (mirror)	**teskatik** (transparent)
kolli (elder man)	**koltik** (bent)

Colors

The majority of color vocabulary words originate with nouns that took the ending -**tik**. Thus, new color terms can always be created as needed.

chipawak	white (literally meaning, clean)
istak	white (literally meaning, like salt)
yayawik	black (from the word yawitl, a type of dark corn)
tliltik	black (like charcoal)
xoxoktik	dark green (from xoxowi, unknown meaning)
xoxowik	green, unripe (from xoxowi, unknown meaning)
tsiktik	blue (like the gum tree)
asultik	blue (from Spanish)
chichiltik	red (like a chili)
kostik	yellow (like a necklace)
tenextli	grey (like ash)
chilkostik	orange (red/yellow)

Color terms can become `light' using the prefix `atl'

achilkostik	light orange
achichiltik	light red

Exercise 29 — Figure out how to form these words using the word bank.

1. spiky _____

2. flowery _____

3. bloody _____

4. young looking woman (based on face) _____

5. indigenous looking face _____

6. non-indigenous looking face _____

7. dark/black in complexion _____

8. round-faced _____

xochitl	flower	**witstli**	thorn
estli	blood	**masewalli**	indigenous, or person
koyotl	non-indigenous, city-raised person, or European	**tliltik/ yayawik**	black
ichpokatl	teenage girl	**tolontli**	root word that means ball, round object
ixtli	implies 'face'		

The word **Koyotl** originally meant a coyote, this is the origin of the English word. With subjugation of Nahuatl communities by Spanish speakers, and given the reputation of coyotes to use trickery to steal animals, the term **koyotl** became synonymous with outsiders. Now, if one wants to refer to coyote the animal, you would have to say **koyochichi**, literally, coyote dog.

In prehispanic times, Nahua citizens were considered to belong to a specific political entity, called the **altepetl** (town, city, government, kingdom etc.). The non-elite class was called 'masewalli', a term that referred to the land rights of citizens of the **altepetl**, so long as they pledged allegiance. Over time, **masewalli** became synonymous with 'indigenous', 'traditional farmers' and with 'the people'.

13.

Past Tense

The next area we must break through deals with the past tense. While not necessarily difficult, this area does have more sound changes we must pay attention to.

Nahuatl verbs belong to one of four different classes. Each class behaves differently in the past tense. There's often no way to tell which class a verb belongs to, so when first learning these, you will have to consult a good dictionary that lays this information out.

Class 1 verbs follow a simple pattern in that they simply add **-k** for the singular, and **-keh** for the plural. No sound changes occur.

Tichoka	`You cry'
Tichokak	`You cried'
Tichokakeh	`We cried'

Class 2 verbs lose the final vowel, and then add **-ki** for the singular, and **-keh** for plurals. However, the deletion of the final vowel will cause consonants to come in contact with each other, and this leads to sound changes. /kk/ can sound like /hk/, but will continue to be spelled /kk/; /wk/ will also sound like /hk/, but will be written /wk/; /yk/ becomes /xk/; /mk/ becomes /nk/. /kw/ can become /wk/.

Tiwetsi	`You fall'
Tiwetski	`You fell'
Tiwetskeh	`We fell'
Tikteki	`You cut it (present tense)'
Tiktekki	`You cut it (past tense)'
Tiktekkeh	`We cut it (past tense)'
Tikchiya	`You wait for him'
Tikchixki	`You waited for him'
Tikchixkeh	`We waited for him'
Tiktsakwa	`You close it'
Tiktsawkki	`You closed it'
Tiktsawkkeh	`We closed it'

Class 3 verbs are the only ones easy to spot. All class 3 verbs end in either **-ia** or **-oa**. To form this past tense, we delete final -a- from the root. Then we add either **-h** or **-hki** for the singular (either is okay); or add **-hkeh** for the plural.

Nimokokoa	`I'm sick'
Nimokokoh	`I got sick'
Nimokokohki	`I got sick'
Timokokohkeh	`We got sick'
Niktlalia	`I place it'
Niktlalih	`I placed it'
Niktlalihki	`I placed it'
Tiktlalihkeh	`We placed it'

Class 4 verbs don't delete any vowels, they simply add **-hki** for the singuar, and **-hkeh** for the plural. Class 4 is the rarest class and very few verbs belong in this category.

Nitlakwa	`I eat'
Nitlakwahki	`I ate'
Titlakwahkeh	`We ate'

This chart below summarizes the endings for the past tense. Of course, the transitive prefixes would only be used on transitive verbs.

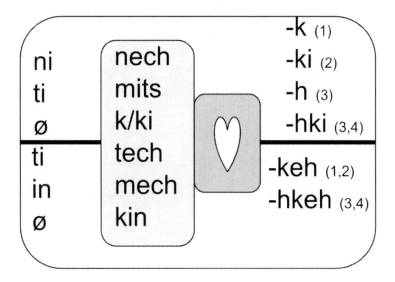

Try to practice actively to better memorize the pattern. While you may need a dictionary at first to recall the class, consistent practice will help you gain fluency without the need for a dictionary. All class -3- verbs are easy to spot with the -ia/-oa endings. Class 4 words are so few they can be memorized. Thus, the biggest distinction is between class 1 and class 2, which can appear to be similar.

Exercise 30 — Tlen kihtosneki?

1. Nikittak _____

2. Tikittakeh _____

3. Kiittakeh _____

4. Intlakwahkeh? _____

5. Ixpoliwkeh _____

6. Mikkeh_____

7. Mikki_____

8. Inmotenxinkeh_____

9. Motenxinki _____

10. Ya nimaltih_____

11. Maltihkeh_____

12. Maltihki_____

13. Maltih_____

14. Intlakwahkeh_____

15. Ya titlakwahkeh_____

16. Mokokohkeh_____

Exercise 31 — Keniwki moillia?

1. You fell _____

2. We fell _____

3. He fell _____

4. They fell _____

5. You woke up _____

6. She woke up_____

7. They woke up_____

8. I got out_____

9. Ya'll got out _____

10. It disappeared_____

11. They disappeared_____

12. You disappeared_____

13. He died_____

14. They died_____

15. I walked_____

16. She ate_____

17. They ate _____

itta	to see (nik) (class 1)	**tlakwa**	to eat (ni) (class 4)
ixpoliwi	for s.t. to disappear (class 2)	**miki**	to die (ni) (class 2)
tenxima	to shave someone (nik) (class 2)	**maltia**	to shower (ni) (class 3)
kokoa	to hurt someone (nik); be sick (nimo); (class 3)	**wetsi**	to fall down (ni) (class 2)
ihsa	to wake up (ni) (class 1)	**kisa**	to leave, exit (ni) (class 2)
nehnemi	to walk (ni) (class 2)	**ya**	already

Central varieties typically use an extra prefix -o- to mark the past tense. They also drop the singular -ki of class 2 verbs.

Onichokak - I cried

Onimitsittak - I saw you

Omokokoh - He got sick

Otiwets - You fell down

ya

By accident, it looks exactly like the Spanish word `ya' of a similar meaning. In Central varieties, the word is pronounced `ye'. The word `ya' can be used in two ways. Firstly, it can be a standalone word. Secondly, it can be a suffix, used at the very end of the verb, even after the tense marker.

Ya nitlakwa
I'm already eating

Nitlakwaya
I'm already eating

Ya nitlakwahki
I already ate

Nitlakwahkiya
I already ate

If it appears next to a consonant, it can change to become more similar. /y/ next to /s/ will become /s/; /y/ next to /k/ will become /k/. Note, recall that the sequence /kk/ can sound like /hk/.

Ya nitlakwas
I'm going to eat already

Nitlakwassa
I'm going to eat already

Juan ya kochtok
Juan is asleep already.

Juan kochtokka
Juan is already asleep

The verb **yaw** `to go' takes an irregular form (**yowa**) when adding -ya.

Niyowa
I'm leaving already.

Take note the difference between verbs ending in -ia and -iya, or -oa and -owa. Native speakers may confuse these since they technically sound nearly identical. However, an -ia or -oa ending will be class 3, and -iya or -owa could be class 1 or 2. Writing the difference will help the readers find it in dictionaries.

maltia > maltih `to shower'         atiya > atixki `to melt'

Greetings

Greetings such as `good day', `good evening' are not typical in Nahua communities. Greetings are used to recognize someone's presence, while also making it obvious that you have no bad intentions by being out on a road. Thus, it is common for people to state the obvious as a greeting (Oh you're cutting grass, hey you're just sitting, hey you're trimming a tree? I'm going there). Below are greetings (G) and responses (R).

Greeting someone on the road, while alone.

G: Neka nionyaw.　　　　　**R: Wenoh.**
I'm heading out.　　　　　　　Okay then.

Greeting on the road, with someone.

G: Neka tionyowih　　　　　**R: Wenoh**
We're heading out　　　　　　Okay then.

Greeting with a handshake.

G: Nimitstlahpalos.　　　　**R: Nimitstlahpalos.**
I greet you.　　　　　　　　　I greet you.

General greeting.

G: Piyali.　　　　　　　　　**R: Piyali.**
Hey/Hi/Bye.　　　　　　　　Hey/Hi/Bye.

Greeting a male by another male on the road.

G: Timomelawah.　　　　　**R: Timomelawah.**
We encounter each other.　　　Later.

Saying goodbye.

G: Timoittaseh　　　　　　**R: Wenoh**
We'll see each other.　　　　　Okay.

G: Mostlayok　　　　　　　**R: Kena mostlayok**
Until tomorrow　　　　　　　Yeah until tomorrow

Leaving home.

G:Ya niyaw/niyowa　　　　**R: Wenoh**
I'm leaving now.　　　　　　　Okay.

Arriving home.

G: Niahsikoya　　　　　　　**R: Wenoh**
I'm home now!　　　　　　　　Okay.

111

Numbers

Number beyond 20 are rarely used by native speakers, and Spanish number are borrowed at that point. It may have lost use given that Mexican currency is based on the *peso* system, which uses a decimal system based on 10, while the Nahuatl language is based on 20. Furthermore, everyday use of *pesos* requires relatively large numbers, which become long words in Nahuatl.

Numbers 6-9 repeat 1-4 segments, only with the addition of **-chikw-**

se	1	**chikwase**	6
ome	2	**chikome**	7
eyi	3	**chikweyi**	8
nawi	4	**chiknawi**	9
makwilli	5 (one handful)	**mahtlaktli**	10 (both hands)

10-14 repeat the system from 10, but 14-20 use a new word based on 15.

mahtlaktli wan se	11	**kaxtolli wan se**	16
mahtlaktli wan ome	12	**kaxtolli wan ome**	17
mahtlaktli wan eyi	13	**kaxtolli wan eyi**	18
mahtlaktli wan nawi	14	**kaxtolli wan nawi**	19
kaxtolli	15	**sempowalli**	20 (one count)

20 to 100 repeat this system, but using sets based 20. **Sempowalli** means `one count, 20'. **Ompowalli** means `two counts, 40'. **Expowalli** means `three counts, 60', etc.

ompowalli	40	**sempowalli wan mahtlaktli**	30 ((1x20))+10)
expowalli	60	**ompowalli wan mahtlaktli**	50 ((2x20))+10)
nawpowalli	80	**expowalli wan mahtlaktli**	70 ((3x20))+10)
makwilpowalli	100	**nawpowalli wan mahtlaktli**	90 ((4x20))+10)

Numbers 100 to 399 follow this same pattern, based on multiples of 20. This continues until we get to 400. The common root for 400 is **sentsontli**. See the breakdown of this word.

sentsontli wan makwilpowalli wan kaxtolli wan nawi (519)

Numbers beyond this are virtually nonexistent in Nahuatl. Historically, the root for the next level of multiplication is xikipilli (8000).

We can use these numbers to state the order of objects.

tlen se - first	**tlen ome** - second
tlen eyi - third	**tlen nawi** - fourth

There's also a separate word that means first: **achtowi**

Numbers take several suffixes. **-kak** refers to place.

senkak - in one place	**onkak** - in two places
exkak - in two places	**nawkak** - in four places

-yok means another, next.

seyok - one more, next

sen- and **sem-** are form of **se** `one'. It implies complete.

senkwa - to eat something all at once
senyowal - all night
semilwitl - all day

Though not used productively in Huasteca, the suffix **-pa** implies `times' in other varieties.

senpa - one time	**ompa** - two times
expa - three times	**nawpa** - four times

Huasteca uses the word **weltah** to mean `times'.

se weltah - one time	**seyok weltah** - next time
ome weltah - two times	**eyi weltah** - three times

Verbal Adjectives

In both Classical and Huasteca varieties we can find a handful of unique verbs that appear to behave like adjectives. These are created by using the prefix **te-** (to people) and the past tense form of a verb (it became X).

kwesoa (for something to make you sad).	tekwesoh that's sad, it's sad (literally, it makes people sad)
kokoa (for something to make you hurt, sick)	tekokoh that hurts! (literally, it hurts people)
mahmawtia (to cause fear in someone)	temahmawtih That's scary, that's dangerous (literally, it causes fear in people)
pakiltia (to make someone happy)	tepakiltih That's happy, it's joyful (literally, it causes happiness in people).
miktia (to kill someone)	temiktih killer, deadly (it kills people)

Se ilwitl tlen tepakiltih. - A happy celebration.

Inon xiwipahtli temahmawtih. - That herb is dangerous.

Tekokoh kemman mitstsopinia. - It hurts when they inject you.

Mikki notlayi. Nopa tekwesoh. - My uncle died. That's sad.

Nopa tekwanih temiktih. - That animal is deadly.

Vocabulary: Days

Nahuatl doesn't have native words for the days of the week, as the modern calendar is a foreign calendar to the Americas and the ancient one fell into disuse. As such, the closest approximations one may find are Nahuatlized pronunciation of Spanish days of the week.

Lones	Monday	**Viernes**	Friday
Martes	Tuesday	**Sabaroh**	Saturday
Miercoles	Wednesday	**Tominkoh**	Sunday
Hoeves	Thursday	**mostla**	tomorrow
wiptlaya	the day before yesterday	**mohmostla**	everyday
yalwaya	yesterday	**wiptla**	the day after tomorrow
ipan kaxtolli	in two weeks	**ipan chikweyi**	in a week (literally 8)
nawyopan	within four days	**kaxtolliya**	two weeks ago
tonatiw	sun, days	**nawyopanya**	three days ago (4, counting today)
metstli	moon, months	**chikweyiya**	a week ago
wahkawkiya	a long time ago	**xiwitl**	year

14.

Noun Endings

There's a few more endings we may commonly find on nouns. We know already of the absolutive endings (**tl, li, in, tli**), the respect/diminutive (**-tsin**), the plural (**-meh**) and the possessive plural (**-wan**), and the inalienable possessive (**-yotl**)

To form nouns from verbs, we can either use **-lli** or **-listli**. -listli implies a process, while -lli implies a result from a process. Remember transitive verbs must be satisfied with the object marker **te/tla** or another noun.

tlahkwilolli
something written

tlahkwilolistli
the act of writing

tlamachtilli
something taught, a lesson

tlamachtilistli
the act of teaching

tlahtolli
something said, word, language

tlahtolistli
the act of talking, speech

We've seen that **-yotl** implies an inalienable possession (**xochitl** flower, **ixochiyo** 'the plant's flower'). When -yotl is used in a non-possessive sentence, it implies an abstraction of that noun, similar to '-ness' in English. These examples are based on Classical Nahuatl.

mexikatl
Aztec, Mexican

mexikayotl
mexicanness

yaotl
enemy

yaoyotl
war

teotl
divine spirit, deity

teoyotl
divinity

If a word is originally a verb, the ending **-kayotl** is used instead.

kwalani
to be angry

kwalankayotl
anger

chiyawa
to be greasy

chiyawakayotl
grease

The ending **-yotl** can change sounds due to contact with other consonants.

tlahtolli `word'	**tlahtollotl** `history'
ekawilli `shade'	**ekawillotl** `shade'
tliltik `black'	**tlillotl** `blackness'

Another ending on nouns is **-yoh**, different from **-yotl**, as **-yoh** implies `full of' or `covered with'.

sokitl mud	**sokiyoh** muddy, dirty
tetl rock	**teyoh** rocky

A few adjectives/adverbs take the ending **-ka** or **-yo** when possessed.

chiyawak greasy	**ichiyawaka** its grease
weweyak long	**iweweyaka/iweweyakayo** its length
wahkapantik tall	**iwahkapanka/iwahkapanyo** its height

In central varieties, there also exists a separate pluralizer for animate nouns, `tin', only used if the word ends in consonant.

totolin `turkey'	**totoltin** `turkeys'
siwatsin `woman (with respect)'	**siwatsitsintin** `women (with respect)'
pilli `child'	**pipiltin** `children'

Exercise 32 — Keniwki moillia?

1. Full of corn _____

2. Full of itch (itchy) _____

3. Full of lice _____

4. Full of grass _____

5. It's weight_____

6. a lie _____

7. a photograph_____

atimitl	lice (note, this will change to atin)	**ahwatl**	an itch
sakatl	grass	**tepetl**	hill
etik	heavy	**elotl**	ripe corn
istlakati	to lie	**ixkopina**	to photograph s.t. (changes to **ixkopin**)

Though rarely used actively today, the ending **-tekatl** is used for naming an inhabitant of a certain town or area that ends in **-tlan**.

Kwextlan
Place of skirts

Kwextekatl
Person from Kwextlan

Tsapotlan
Place of sapote fruit

Tsapotekatl
Person from Tsapotlan

Mixtlan
Place of clouds

Mixtekatl
Person from Mixtlan

The ending **-mekatl** was used to identify people from a region ending in **-man**.

Chichiman
Place of milk, suckling, or dogs (depends on vowel length)

Chichimekatl
Person from Chichiman

Vocabulary: Wild Animals

tekwani	wild animal	**newktsin**	bee
tototl	bird	**etsatl**	wasp
koyochichi	coyote	**masatl**	deer
tlakwachin/ tlakwakilotl	possum	**pesohtli**	coatimundi
mapachin	raccoon	**kimichin**	mouse, rat
michin	fish	**kwawtli**	eagle
okwilin	worm	**totolin**	turkey
tekolotl	owl	**palach**	male turkey
tokatl	spider	**koatl**	snake

Exercise 33 — Keniwki moillia?

1. I saw an owl.

2. Did you see that spider?

3. I'm observing the eagle.

4. Grab that mouse!

5. The snake is eating a mouse.

itta	to see something (nik) (class 1)	**tlakwa**	to eat in general (ni) (class 4)
tlachilia	to observe something (nik) (class 3)	**kwa**	to eat something specific (nik) (class 4)
itskia	to grab something (nik) (class 3)	**inon**	that

Tekwanimeh

Across
2. bee
4. coyote
5. deer
7. snake
8. bird

Down
1. coatimundi
3. owl
6. spider

Conversation

Marta: Piyali Luz, tikkwa tlaxkalli?

Luz: Kena, timasewalmeh tikkwah miak tlakwalistli ika sintli.

Luz: Wan yeka moneki ma timiltekitikan.

Luz: Sanpampa onkah miak tekwanimeh tlen kinekih kikwaseh tlatoktli.

Marta: Nelliya? Katlinya?

Luz: Masameh, pesohmeh, nohkiya sekin tlamantli totomeh.

Marta: Keniwki inkimanawia milli?

Luz: Kemman selik konetoktli, se masewalli kitlachilia milli.

Marta: Ah inon miak tekitl.

Luz: Kena, sanpampa sintli toessoh, tlawel ipatiw.

tlaxkalli	tortilla	yeka	that's why
tlakwalistli	anything edible	moneki	it's necessary
sintli	corn	miltekiti	to work the field
sanpampa	however	tlatoktli	something planted
katlinya	which?	nelliya	true
manawia	to defend something (nik)	milli	agricultural field
selik	fresh, green, ripe	konetoktli	baby corn sprout
tlachilia	to observe something (nik)	kwa	to eat something (nik)
Tlawel ipatiw.	It has a lot of value.		

15.

Noun and Verb Compounds

In this section, we'll cover common compounds that can attach onto nouns and verbs. Firstly, recall that transitive verbs must be satisfied with an object prefix. An alternative to this is to incorporate a noun directly in the place of the object prefix, a process called *noun incorporation*.

Toka means `to plant something'

Niktoka xochitl
I plant flowers

Nixochitoka
I plant flowers

Niktoka etl
I plant beans

Nietoka
I plant beans

Saka means `to transport something'

Niksaka sintli
I transport corn

Nisinsaka
I transport corn

Niksaka kwawitl
I transport firewood

Nikwasaka
I transport firewood

Namaka means `to sell something'

Niknamaka pitsotl
I sell pigs

Nipitsonamaka
I sell pigs

Niknamaka chilli
I sell chili

Nichilnamaka
I sell chili

Kwa means `to eat something'

Nikkwa elotl
I eat fresh corn

Nielokwa
I eat fresh corn

Nikkwa nakatl
I eat meat

Ninakakwa
I eat meat

Teki means `to cut s.t., or, to harvest s.t.'

Nikteki etl
I harvest beans

Nieteki
I harvest beans

Nikteki xochitl
I cut flowers

Nixochiteki
I cut flowers

A common pair of compounding prefixes for nouns are **kwa** (wooden, wild, or head) and **tepos** (metallic).

kwapuertah
wooden door

kwapitsotl
wild pig

kwatochin
wild rabbit

kwaestli
tree sap

kwachichiltik
red hair

kwasesoh
brains

teposkawayoh
bicycle

tepostototl
airplane

Adding any two nouns together is generally straightforward, but note that the first noun modifies the second noun. For example, **kwaestli** is a type of `blood' (**estli**) of the type `tree' (**kwa**). If we switch the order, we would be stating **eskwawitl**, meaning `a kind of tree' of the type `estli' blood, kind of like saying `blood-like tree', instead of `tree-like blood'. Incidentally, **eskwawitl** happens to be a real type of medicinal tree.

xochikoskatl
a necklace of the type `flower'
a flowery necklace

siwatototl
a bird of the type `female'
a female bird

atototl
a bird of the type `water'
a water bird

tsopelatl
water of the type `sweet'
sweet water

It's easiest to add two simple nouns together. Nouns modified into agentives, for example, cannot generally be attached. Agentives and verbs could take the abstract -**ka** before allowing compounding onto a noun, though its not common.

*momachtianikalli
*student house

momachtikakalli
student house

In rare cases can you do the reverse (**kaltlamachtihketl** = teacher's building, school). Finally, verbs can attach onto verbs using the morpheme -**ka**. Again, the first verb acts as the modifier to the second verb.

mawi
to fear

tlahtoa
to speak

mawkatlahtoa
he speaks with fear

tlasoa
to love (ancient form)

mati
to know

tlasohkamati
to appreciate, give thanks

123

Exercise 34 — Keniwki moillia?

1. I plant sweet potato _____

2. I transport water _____

3. I sell corn _____

4. I cut trees _____

5. I drink medicine _____

6. I sell medicine _____

7. Internet _____

8. male dog _____

9. male cat _____

10. female cat _____

11. zapote fruit tree _____

12. orange fruit tree _____

13. banana tree _____

14. I'm lazy (dying from lazyness)_____

kamohtli	sweet potato, yam	**saka**	to transport something (nik)
sintli	corn	**kwawitl**	trees (becomes kwa as a prefix)
pahtli	medicine	**oni**	to drink something
namaka	to sell something	**tepostli**	metal
tokatsawalli	spider web	**okichtli**	male animal
siwatl	female	**tsapotl**	zapote fruite
alaxox	orange	**kwaxilotl**	banana
tlatsiwi	to be lazy (ni) (becomes tlats)	**miki**	to die (ni)

Conjunctions

Below are a list of common conjunctions in Huasteca Nahuatl.

so (or)
Niktekiwis kawayoh so borroh.
I'll use a horse or donkey.

sanpampa (however); **pero** (but)
Nikochmiki sanpampa/pero moneki nitekitis.
I'm sleepy but I have to work.

Yon (not even, nor)
Axnikkwas kwaxilotl yon alaxox.
I won't eat bananas nor oranges.

Subordinate conjunctions such as `before, after, simultaneously' are not preferred structures in Nahuatl. Nahuatl avoids this by saying `X happened, then Y', instead of `X happened before Y'. Nahuatl also avoids comparatives and superlatives (big, bigger, biggest) and instead uses the structure (X is big, Y is not).

wankinon (`and then', emphasizing time)
Juan kipantih tomin, wankinon kikowki se jarana.
`Juan found money, and then he bought a *jarana* guitar.

wakka (`and thus' emphasizing reason)
Tlanki notomin, wakka tlen tikchiwaseh?
I finished my money, so then what are we going to do?

yeka (`that's why')
Tlaonik cheneh, yeka iwintik.
He drank too much, that's why he's drunk.

maskeh/mewkatsan (even though)
Maskeh kionik axkwalli pahtli, amo mikki.
Even though he drank poison, he didn't die.

noke (meanwhile)
Xitlachpana noke nitlapahpakas
You sweep while I wash the dishes!

The construction `As soon as', is developed by using **san** with the directional -**on**- in the verb.
San nitlakwas wan tionyaseh.
As soon as I eat we'll go.

Relative Pronouns

The most common relative pronoun is **tlen,** meaning `he who, she who, those who, that which'.

> **tlen wikah**
> those who sing, singers

> **Tlamachtihketl tlen kwachokox wallas.**
> The teacher with blond hair is coming. (literally: the teacher who is blond haired)

> **se siwatl tlen ixmasewaltik**
> a woman with indigenous facial features

> **Nikittak ne okichpil tlen mokokoh.**
> I saw that boy who was sick.

> **Ne okichpil tlen mokokoh kochtok.**
> That boy who is sick is asleep.

In some towns in the Huasteca, the relativizer `**ankeh**' is used for relativizing only people.

> **ankeh wikah**
> those who sing

In Classical Nahuatl, the particle `**in**' can be used as a relativizer.

> **in kwikwah**
> those who sing (Classical uses kwika instead of wika)

> **in kochtokeh siwah**
> the sleeping women

These were the most common relativizers in Nahuatl, though specific region may use different relativizers, including `**tlen, in, on, in tlen, tlin,** or a form of **inon: on, non**.

Tlen vs. Para

In the Huasteca, the word **para** was borrowed from Spanish, typically meaning `in order that'.

> **Xiwallaw para nimitsittas.**
> Come so I may see you.

> **Para ta.**
> For you.

> **Para timoskaltis, moneki xitlakwa kwalli.**
> In order for you to grow, you need to eat well.

Para also has a unique use in Huasteca Nahuatl, as it is used to introduce a subordinate clause. The difference between `para' and `tlen' can cause much confusion for Nahuatl learners, since both can sound like the word `que' in Spanish. Recall that **tlen** best means `he/she/they who', while **para** introduces a new clause, especially a statement or hypothesis.

> **Kihtoa *para* axwallas.**　　**Axwallas tlen wika.**
> He said *that* he won't come.　[He who sings] won't come.

> **Niktlalia para amo tlaawetsis.**
> I think that it won't rain.

Para, when used to subordinate a clause, can be optional.

> **Kihtoa axwallas.**
> He said he won't come.

> **Niktlalia amo tlaawetsis.**
> I think it won't rain.

Students often comment on how Nahuatl has taken borrowings from foreign languages, most notably Spanish. On the one hand, the conditions under which borrowing occurred were harsh periods of occupation and colonization. On the other hand, all languages of the world have borrowings. Most of English vocabulary doesn't even come from English, yet this doesn't hinder the power of English.

Vocabulary: Class 1 Verbs

tlatla	for something to burn	**temo**	to climb down (ni)
tlastla	to care for something with jealousy (nik)	**tlehko**	to climb up (ni)
toka	to plant something, to plant, to bury someone (ni) or (nik)	**tona**	for it to be sunny
tsahtsi	to shout or cry	**choka**	to cry (ni)
kwi	to grab something (nik)	**wetska**	to laugh (ni)
maka	to give something to someone (nik)	**patla**	to change something (nik); for something to change (mo)
ixtemo	to climb downhill	**ixtlehko**	to climb uphill

Exercise 35: **Match**

1. tsahtsik	**a.** I already gave it
2. tsahtsiseh	**b.** We already gave it
3. nikmakakka	**c.** I changed it
4. tikmakakehya	**d.** It changed
5. kikwik	**e.** he grabbed it
6. kikwikeh	**f.** they grabbed it
7. niwetskak	**g.** She laughed
8. wetskak	**h.** I laughed
9. mopatlak	**i.** They will shout
10. nikpatlak	**j.** He shouted

Vocabulary: Class 2 Verbs

mati	to know something (nik)	**kawa**	to leave something (nik); for something to be left (mo); for someone to be left (nimo)
miki	to die (ni)	**kalaki**	to enter (ni)
kaki	to hear something (nik)	**chichina**	to suck something, to smoke (nik)
chiwa	to do/make something (nik)	**chiya**	to wait for someone (nik); to wait (nimo)
kochi	to sleep (ni)	**kowa**	to buy something (nik)
kwalani	to be mad (ni)	**weli**	to be able (ni)
wetsi	to fall down (ni)	**piya**	to have something

Exercise 36: **Match**

1. mokawki   a. We entered

2. mokawkeh   b. You entered

3. tikalakki   c. Yes it's possible

4. tikalakkeh   d. I can't do it

5. nitlachichinki   e. They smoked

6. tlachichinkeh   f. I smoked

7. kena weli   g. They were left behind

8. axniweli   h. It was left

9. kipixki   i. We had it

10. tikpixkeh   j. He had it

16.

Verb Tenses

So far we've learned about the present, future and past tense verbs. The rest of the verb tenses are generally straightforward rules with little to no irregularities.

Conditional Tense

The conditional tense is used to express what you `would have done' or what you `should have done but couldn't', or `would do hypothetically'. The singular form is **-skia**, and the plural ending is -**skiah**. Delete the final -**a**- in **ia/oa** verbs.

Nitekitiskia tlan niweliskia.
I would work if I could.

Nitekitiskia pero axniwelki.
I would have worked but I wasn't able to.

Tiyaskiah tlan timoahxiliskiah.
We would go if we had time.

Tlan onkaskia sintli titlaxkalchiwaskiah
If we had corn we would make tortillas

Imperfect Tense

The imperfect tense describes what you `used to do' or what you `were doing'. Eliminate the final vowel in **-ia/oa** verbs again before you add the ending **-yaya** (for the singular) or **-yayah** (for the plural).

Nitekitiyaya.　　　　　　**Titekitiyayah.**
I used to work.　　　　　　We used to work.

Nimomachtiyaya kemman nechnotski nonanan.
I was working when my mom called me.

Nimotlaloyaya　　　　　　**Nimotlaloyaya.**
I used to run.　　　　　　I was running.

Perfect Tenses

The verb particle **-to-** exists in four forms `tok', `tos', `toskia' and `toya', related to the past, future, conditional, and imperfect tenses, in order. Again, **-ia-** and **-oa-** endings will lose the final **-a**.

> **-Tok** (singular) and **-tokeh** (plural) imply what `has happened'; the Past Perfect. This tense can sometimes imply the present tense (being in state of x), often for for positional verbs.

Nimosewih. I sat down.

Nimosewihtok. I have sat down. I'm in a state of sitting.

Mokawa. It gets left behind

Mokawtok. It has been left behind.

Nikkwa inin tlakwalli. I eat this food.

Tikkwahtok inin tlakwalli? Have you eaten this food before?

Kochtok. He's asleep (in a state of sleeping).

Tlakwahtokeh. They are eating right now (In a state of eating).

Ahketstok - He's laying on his back.

Ihkatokeh - They are standing (in a standing position).

Kaki - to hear something

Nikkaktok - I have heard it before.

Eltok se amoxtli. - Here's a book.

Itstok se tenantsin. An elder lady is present.

Nikitta se amoxtli - I see a book.

Nikitstok ne amoxtli. - I have seen that book before.

> **-Tos** (singular) and **-toseh** (plural) are used for the future perfect, stating: `what you will be doing when X is happening'. These endings can also be applied with positional verbs.

Amo xiwallaw tlayowa, nitlakwatos. Don't come in the evening, I will be eating (at that time).

Momaihtotoseh tiopan mostla. Tomorrow they will have been praying in church.

Yoltos seyok ichkatl. Another sheep will be alive.

Mosewitoseh masewalmeh. The men will have been sitting down.

Amo niitstos. I won't be here.

Axtiitstoseh. We won't be here.

Ihkatos. He will be standing.

Ihkatoseh. They will be standing.

Kochtos. She will be sleeping.

Miktoseh. They will be dead.

-**Toya** (singular) and **-toyah** (plural) are used for the past perfect progressive, stating: what you `had been doing'.

Niitstoya ipan kaltlamachtiloyan. I had been at school.

Titlakwatoyah. We had been eating.

Kochtoya. She had been asleep (at that time).

Kochtoyah. They had been asleep (at that time).

Niyahtoya altepetl. I had gone to the City.

Tsawktoya. It had been closed.

-**Toskia** (singular) and **-toskiah** (plural) are used for the conditional perfect, stating: what `would have happened, but didn't. It's similar to **-skia** but with a slight difference. For the most part the two are interchangeable. See below.

Miktoskia. He would have been dead (but didn't)

Mikiskia. He would have died.

Wetstoskia. She would have fallen (but didn't).

Wetsiskia. She would fall.

Kikowtoskia tixtli. She would have bought dough, but didn't.

Kikowaskia tixtli. She would have bought dough. She would buy dough (if X happens).

All the conjugations of kochi, using (you) and (we).

tikochiyaya	tikochiyayah
tikochiskia	tikochiskiah
tikochtok	tikochtokeh
tikochtos	tikochtoseh
tikochtoya	tikochtoyah
tikochtoskia	tikochtoskiah

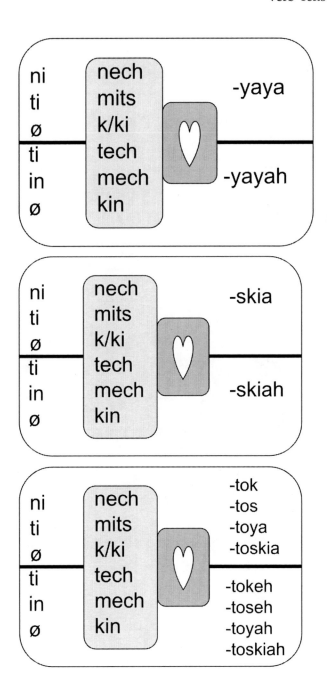

Exercise 37 — Tlen kihtosneki?

1. Nechpaxaloskia, pero axmoahxilia

_____

2. Nimitstlaxtlawiliskia pero axonkah tomin

_____

3. Nikkowaskia tlan nikpiyaskia tomin

_____

4. Tiktlachiliskiah tlamawisolli pero ya axkineki.

_____

5. Tiktlachiliyayah tlamawisolli _____

6. Nikoniyaya chichik _____

7. Kanin eltok noyaves? _____

8. Eltos yankwik tlamawisolli_____

9. Eltoya se amoxtli, pero axnikahsi _____

10. Ayokkana tiihkatoseh _____

paxaloa	to visit someone (nik)	**ahxilia**	to be free, available, have time (nimo)
kowa	to buy something (nik)	**onkah**	to exist
piya	to have something (nik)	**tlaxtlawilia**	to pay someone (nik)
tomin	money	**tlachilia**	to observe something (nik)
tlamawisolli	t.v.; show; video	**neki**	to want something (nik)
oni	to drink something (nik)	**chichik**	alcohol, beer
yaves	keys	**yankwik**	new
ahsi	to find something (nik)	**ihka**	to be standing (ni)

Exercise 38 — Keniwki moillia?

1. I would do it if I could_____

2. I would eat if I were hungry_____

3. We would stay if we weren't busy _____

4. I was eating when you called me _____

5. We used to watch t.v. _____

6. I would sleep now but I can't _____

7. They used to sleep early, not anymore_____

8. He is asleep _____

9. He will be asleep if you call him_____

10. She had been asleep when you called her _____

chiwa	to do something (nik)	**weli**	to be able to do something , can, could (ni)
kwa	to eat something (nik); to eat in general (nitla)	**mayana**	to be hungry (ni)
kawa	to stay (nimo)	**tekiwia**	to be busy (nimo)
tlachilia	to watch, observe (nik)	**nohnotsa**	to call someone (nik)
kochi	to sleep (ni)	**niman**	soon, early

Vocabulary: Class 3 Verbs

ihkwiloa	to write something (nik)	ihtoa	to say something (nik)
illia	to tell someone something (nik)	saniloa	to talk (ni)
maltia	to bathe (ni)	altia	to bathe someone (nik)
sewia	to cool something off (nik); to sit down (nimo)	selia	to receive something
mawiltia	to play (ni)	awiltia	to play with something (nik)
kwesoa	for something to worry one (nech); to be sad (nimo)	machilia	to feel something (nik)
mihtotia	to dance (ni)	ihtotia	to make something dance (nik)
machtia	to study (nimo); to teach (nitla)	miktia	to kill someone (nik)
mihyotia	to have a smell, good or bad (ni)	neltokilia	to believe someone, something (nik)
paktia	to make someone happy, or laugh; or laugh at someone (nik)	palewia	to help someone (nik)
pantia	to unexpectedly find something (nik)	kixtia	to take out (nik)
temoa	to find something (nik)	tlahpaloa	to greet someone (nik)

Recall that /**mo**/ is the reflexive. At times, the -**o**- can be swallowed by a verb that starts with a vowel, as in (**moaltia > maltia**). This means the real root of **maltia** is actually **altia**, it just has the -**mo**- fused when used reflexively.

Exercise 39: **Match**

1. **Xikselih ni koskatl.**	**a.** Don't kill it yet.
2. **Nimitstlahpalos.**	**b.** Receive this necklace.
3. **Xinechpalewi.**	**c.** Take a bath already.
4. **Ximaltiya.**	**d.** Who will help me?
5. **Nechpaktia nimaltis.**	**e.** Help me.
6. **Nechpaktia nimihtotis.**	**f.** I greet you.
7. **Ayikana xikmikti.**	**g.** I like to dance.
8. **Amo nechneltokilia.**	**h.** I like to shower.
9. **Tlen tikmachilia?**	**i.** She doesn't believe me.
10. **Akkiya nechpalewis?**	**j.** What do you feel?

Vocabulary: Class 4 Verbs

The list of Class 4 verbs in the whole language is quite small. These are the majority below. Of course, there are derivations of these verbs (**nakakwa** `to eat meat', **sinkwa** `to eat corn', **elokwa** `to eat fresh corn', **ekwa** `to eat beans' etc.).

kwa	to eat something (nik); to eat in general (nitla)	**nawa**	to carry something with your shoulders (nik)
mama	to carry something on your back (nik)	**nahnawa**	to hug someone (nik)
pa	to paint something (nik)	**ixpa**	to put makeup on someone (nik)
tlankwa	to bite yourself (nimo); to grab something with one's teeth (nik)	**ya**	to go (ni)

Word Order

You may have noticed Nahuatl is not strict with word order. The prefixes and suffixes on verbs plus context are considered enough to make it clear who is doing the action and who is receiving the action. As such, Nahuatl has relatively free word order.

Ne okichpil kiittak se chichi.
That boy saw a dog. (emphasis on subject: the boy)

Kiittak se chichi ne okichpil.
That boy saw a dog. (emphasis on action: he saw)

Se chichi kiittak ne okichpil.
That boy saw a dog. (emphasis on object: dog)

Ancient Nahuatl had a tendency to use the verb first, followed by either the subject or object. Modern Huasteca continues to be heavily Verb-first, but equally allows subjects to be first. The one selected first may receive extra emphasis.

Not surprisingly, adjectives can go either before or after the noun it modifies.

Nikpixtok se miston yayawik.
I have a black cat.

Nikpixtok se yayawik miston.
I hav a black cat.

The biggest difference with English lies in its seemingly floating particles, for example /**ika**/.

Nomacheteh tlen ika nitlateki
My machete with which I cut.

Nomacheteh ika tlen nitlateki.
My machete with which I cut.

Nomacheteh tlen nitlateki ika.
My machete with which I cut.

The preposition **pan** or **ipan** typically goes before the noun as we've seen, but not after a noun. However, when used with a verb, it can precede the verb. **Pan** can also come after the verb, typically if its present with a noun. Also, these particle words took possessive pronouns in ancient Nahuatl, but these are now optional.

pan tlalli	***tlalli pan**
on the land	*on the land
pan ichan	***ichan pan**
at her house	*at her house
Mosewia pan kwasiyah.	**Pan mosewia.**
She sits on the chair.	She sits on it.
Mosewia ipan kwasiya.	**Ipan mosewia.**
He sits on the chair.	He sits on it.

The word /**wanya**/ `together with' behaves the same as /**pan**/, going before or after the verb.

Mawiltia iwanya Leti.	**Iwanya mawiltia.**
He plays with Leti.	He plays with her.
Mawiltia wanya Leti.	**Wanya mawiltia.**
He plays with Leti.	He plays with Leti.
Wanya nemi Julio.	**Nemi wanya Julio.**
He hangs out with Julio.	He hangs out with Julio.

Tlen ika is actually one of several dual particles in Nahuatl. These words can mean different things individually, but when combined give rise to a new meaning. You may see these written as one word.

tlen ika what with	that with which
san tekitl just work	done in any way
san kwalli just good	just right, matching someone perfectly
san sampa just again	all at once
san sehko just united	together
san niman just soon	right after

17.

Directionality

Verbs can also take prefixes that indicate the direction an action is done. The two directional prefixes are **-on-** and **-wal-**. **On-** implies an action is done `toward there', and it can also be used to imply an action done right away, quickly.

>**Xionyaw** - Go towards there!

>**Xionyaw** - Go quickly!

Wal- implies an action is done `toward here'.

>**Xiwalkochi** - Come sleep toward here!

>**Walmotekas** - He's laying down toward here.

Note that these directionals are placed after the subject and object prefixes, but before the reflexive `**mo**'. Below is a summary of the verb prefixes and suffixes we've seen thus far.

Negation	Subject Pronouns	Object Pronouns	Directional	Reflexive	Non-Specific	Root	Tense & Plural Or Directional	Already
	ni-	nech					-k/-ki/-hki	
	ti-	mits					-s	
ax-	Ø-	k/ki	on		te		-skia	
ayi-				mo			-tok/tos/-toya	-ya
ayok-	ti-	tech			tla		-h	
	in-	mech	wal				-keh/-hkeh	
	Ø-	kin					-seh	
							-tokeh/toseh/toyah	
							-skiah	

Axnimitsontlamakak.

I didn't feed you (in that direction).

Ayoknechwaltlaskamatiliskia.

He won't thank me any more (towards here).

There are no grammatical restrictions on using -**on**- or -**wal**-, that is to say, they can be used with any tense, with singular or plurals, or with transitives or intransitives. This remains true so long as the directional meaning is intended of course.

Konittas iichpokaw - She's going to see her daughter.

Kontlaskamatilih iweltiw - He went to thank his granddaughter.

Kiwalmanaskia tlaxkalli pero axkipiya tixtli. She would come to place tortillas (on the griddle) but she doesn't have dough.

The directional -**on**- gave birth to the verb -**oni**- `to drink something'. The original root of `to drink' is /**I**/. This has led to the following synonyms.

Nitlai - I drink stuff

Nitlaoni - I drink stuff.

The directional -**wal**- gave birth to the distinction between **wika** `to take' and **walwika** (written as **wallika**) `to bring'. Note that **xikwika** is pronounced xih-wi-ka.

Xikwika ne chikiwitl - Take that basket.

Xikwallika ne chikiwitl - Bring that basket.

Consider the verb `**kaki**', which means `to listen to something'. When it takes the prefix **tla**, it now means **tlakaki** `to listen in general, to obey'. It can also take an extra form `**tlakakilia**' which means `to obey someone'. The transitive verb **kaki** becomes satisfied when it becomes **tlakaki**, however, it becomes a new unsatisfied transitive verb as **tlakakilia**, and it now requires a new object prefix.

Nimitskaki. - I hear you.

Nitlakaki. - I hear things, I obey.

Nimitstlakakilia. - I listen to you. I obey you.

Directional Purposive

There's one more set of directionals in Nahuatl. However, they operate with several differences from the general directionals. For one, they are suffixes, not prefixes to the verb root. Secondly, they take over the spot for verb tenses since they actually imply tense. Lastly, these second directionals imply `traveling with the purpose of doing verb X'.

-ti	`toward there, in the future'	**-to**	`toward there, in the past'
-ki	`toward here, in the future'	**-ko**	`toward here, in the past'.

To help us memorize these forms, note that both **ki** and **ko** have a **k** and imply `toward here'. Similarly, both **ti** and **to** share the implication `toward there'. On the other hand, both **to** and **ko** are in the past, and both **ti** and **ki** are in the future. Here's some examples.

Nitlakwati.	I will go there in order to eat.
Nitlakwato.	I went there in order to eat.
Nitlakwaki.	I will come here in order to eat.
Nitlakwako.	I came here in order to eat.

To pluralize, simply add **-h** onto any of these four.

Titlakwatih.	We will go there to eat.
Titlakwatoh.	We went there to eat.
Titlakwakih.	We will come here to eat.
Titlakwakoh.	We came here to eat.

With these directional purposives, we also delete **-a** from **-ia/-oa** endings.

Kitemoti.	He's going in order to look for it.
Mihtotiti.	He's going in order to dance.

You cannot use a tense with these directionals, it's one or the other.

*****Nitlakwatis**	*I will go to eat.

Exercise 40 — Tlen kihtosneki?

1. Nikontekis manko_____

2. Mohmostla nikwalteki manko_____

3. Xikontisi sintli_____

4. Ma tikontisikan sintli _____

5. Momachtiti_____

6. Momachtito _____

7. Momachtiki_____

8. Momachtiko_____

9. Momachtikoh_____

10. Amo ximomachtiti_____

Exercise 41 — Keniwki moillia?

1. She went (over there) in order to sell stuff_____

2. I came (here) in order to sell stuff _____

3. We came (here) in order to buy stuff_____

4. Tomorrow I will come (here) in order to buy stuff_____

5. Tomorrow they will come (here) in order to sleep_____

6. I'm going (over there) in order to sleep_____

7. I'm going to sleep (over there) _____

8. Go (over there) to call your dad_____

teki	to cut s.t. (nik)	**manko**	mango
tisi	to grind s.t. (nik)	**sintli**	corn
namaka	to sell s.t. (nik)	**kowa**	to buy s.t. (nik)
mostla	tomorrow	**kochi**	to sleep (ni)
notsa	to call s.o. (nik)	**momachtia**	to study (ni)

Vocabulary: Dressing Yourself

piki	to cover oneself, such as with a blanket or sweater (nik/nimo)	**patsmiktia**	for clothes to make you warm (nech)
ompanoa	to put a second layer of clothing on (nik/nimo)	**patla**	to change s.t. or s.o. (nik/nimo)
pahpatla	to change frequently.	**xolotik**	nude person
pepestik	nude person	**yoyontia**	to put clothes on someone (nik/nimo)
namiki	for clothing to match or go well with someone (nech)	**kwi**	for clothing to fit someone, in terms of size (nech)
kwelpachoa	to fold clothes (nik)	**ganchohwia**	to hang clothes on a hook (nik)
yoyomitl	clothes	**kotomitl**	shirt, blouse
kweitl	dress	**kotonsosol**	old clothes
pestetl	diaper	**koskatl**	necklace
tekaktli	shoes	**kotontia**	to dress someone (nik/nimo)
kwakwi	for a hat to fit (nech)	**ikxikwi**	for shoes to fit (nech)
kixtilia	to undress (nimo)	**pantalonkixtia**	to take off pants (nimo)

Keep in mind that when the object of clothing does an action toward you, it makes sense to use the object prefix **nech** (to me). When you are the one doing the action to yourself, it makes sense to use **nimo** (I to myself).

Namiki has many meanings, but they are all tied to its original meaning of `things matching each other, meeting each other, encountering each other'. Thus, you are literally saying `the clothes encounter me, match me'. With **kwi** you imply `they grab me'.

Many nouns with the ending sequence -**mitl** become -**n** when possessed. This is because the /i/ is weak, leaving the /m/ at the end. However, Nahuatl sound rules don't allow /m/ at the end of words, so it becomes /n/. Finally, word final /n/ is often a soft /h/ sound. This is how **kotomitl** `shirt' can sound like /nokotoh/ `my shirt'.

If **yoyomitl** means `clothes', can you figure out how to say `my clothes'?

145

18.

Auxiliary Verbs

Nahuatl, like many Uto-Aztecan languages, makes use of sequences combining two verbs. Nahuatl employs only a relatively small group of auxiliary verb endings that can attach to any verb, each with its own meaning. Note they are all attached with the help of a *ligature* -**ti**-. It's also important to know that these endings can take a tense ending, with the exception of -**tikah** which means `right now'. If you use a tense ending, modify the verb root as if it were changing to the past tense (i.e. note if it's Class 1,2,3,4).

-tikah/tikateh	To be in a state of doing an action; right now.
-tinemi/tinemih	To do an action here and there and everywhere.
-tiwallaw/tiwallowih	To do an action continuously toward here.
-tiw/tiyowih	To do an action continuously toward there.
-tewa/-tewah	To do something before leaving. When used with **choka** (cry) or **wetska** (laugh) it intensifies the action.
-tikisa/-tikisah	To do an action while on the way somewhere.
-tiwetsi/tiwetsih	To have just done something. To do something suddenly.
-tihkak/-tihkakeh	To remain (literally, to be standing)

tikah/tikateh

Tlakwahtikah. He's eating right now.

Titlakwahtikateh. We're eating right now.

tinemi/tinemih

Chokatinemi. She's crying here and there.

Chokatinemiyaya. She was crying all over the place.

Tichokatinemis. You're going to be crying all over.

Nehnentinemih. They are walking all about.

146

tiwallaw/tiwallowih

Mihtotihtiwallaw. He comes along dancing.

Mihtotihtiwallowih. They come along dancing.

Tlakwahtiwallayaya. She was eating on the way here.

Tlakwahtiwallahkeh. They ate while on the way here.

tiw/tiyowih

Mihtotihtiw. - He goes along dancing.

Mihtotihtis. - He's going to go along while dancing.

Chokatiyaseh. - They will go along while crying.

Tlanamakatiyaskia. - He would go along selling (but didn't).

tewa/tewah

Xikonitewa wan tiyaseh - Drink it and we'll take off.

Nikkwatewas. - I'm going to eat it (before leaving).

tikisa/tikisah

Kixotlatikiski. - The car hit it (while going away).

Kiitskihtikiskeh - They took it (while going away).

tiwetsi/tiwetsih

Techtlankwahtiwetsi. - He suddenly bites us.

Nechtlankwahtiwetski. - He suddenly bit me.

Mitsmahmawtihtiwetsiseh. - They will suddenly scare you.

tihkak/tihkakeh

Itstihkak. - He continues existing (related to itstok).

Ihkatihkayaya - It used to exist (standing) (for example, a tree).

Kochtihkaskia. - He would remain sleeping (but couldn't).

Exercise 42 — Tlen kihtosneki?

1. Nechnotstiwallaw_____

2. Nechnotstiw_____

3. Kikwahtiwetski_____

4. Tlakwahtikah_____

5. Tlakwahtihkak_____

6. Tlaonitinemi_____

7. Nikkowatewas_____

8. Kikwahtikiski_____

notsa	to call out to someone (nik) (class 2)	**tsahtsi**	to yell, scream (ni) (class 1)
kwa	to eat something (nik) (class 4)	**kikisi**	to whistle (ni) (class 2)
nohnotsa	to call someone (class 2)	**momachtia**	to learn, study (ni) (class 3)
oni	to drink something (nik) (class 1)	**nehnemi**	to walk (ni) (class 2)
kowa	to buy something (nik) (class 2)	**wika**	to sing (ni) (class 1)

Exercise 43 — Keniwki moillia?

1. She's singing [here and there]_____

2. They are singing [here and there] _____

3. They were walking [here and there]_____

4. He's studying right now. _____

5. They're studying right now._____

6. She comes whistling. _____

7. She goes whistling. _____

8. She suddenly screamed. _____

Helping Verbs

Three common helping verbs are not attached like the (-ti) forms. These are **weli** (to be able), **tlami** (to finish) and **pewa** (to start). What makes these three unique is that they don't have to be conjugated to match other verbs in terms of *person*. Thus, these two forms are possible.

Nitlanki nitlakwa
I finished eating.

Tlanki nitlakwa
I finished eating (finished is the act of me eating).

Nipewas nitekitis
I'll start working.

Pewas nitekitis
I'll start working (starting is the act of me working).

Niweli nikwatlehkos.
I can climb a tree.

Weli nikwatlehkos.
I can climb a tree (the act of me climbing trees is possible).

You may be unsure of the right tense to use on either the helping verb or the main verb. In **Nitlanki nitlakwa**, the act is finished, so why isn't `eating' in the past tense? This is because using both would produce two separate and odd sentences, something like this below.

> *Nitlanki nitlakwahki.
> I finished I ate.

However, it is permissible for one or both to be in the future tense.

Nitlamis nimomachtis
I will finish studying

Nitlamis nimomachtia
I will finish studying.

Exercise 44 — Keniwki moillia?

1. I'll start reading (tlapowa, class 2)_____

2. I finished reading (tlapowa, class 2)_____

3. I'll start writing (tlahkwiloa, class 3)_____

4. I finished writing (tlahkwiloa, class 3)_____

5. She can write (tlahkwiloa, class 3)_____

Vocabulary: At The Store

namaka	to sell something (nik) (class 1)	**kowa**	to buy something (nik) (class 2)
namakiltia	to sell something to someone	**kowia**	to buy something for someone (nik) (class 3)
patiyoh	expensive	**kowilia**	to buy something from/for someone (nik) (class 3)
keski ipatiw?	What is its value? How much is it?	**litroh**	means 'liters' in Spanish, but can mean 'pounds' in Huasteca marketplaces.
tlen moneki	what is necessary? How can I help you?	**tomin**	money
pesoh	Mexican pesos	**tlanamakaketl**	vendor
tlawika	to owe in general (ni) (class 1)	**tlanewtia**	to lend something to someone (nik) (class 3)
tlawikilia	to owe someone (nik) (class 3)	**tlanewi**	to borrow something (nimo); to hire someone (nik) (class 2)
pitsawak	thin; coins/loose change	**tlaxtlawi**	to pay (class 2)
		tlaxtlawilia	to pay s.o. (class 3)

Try to read this short narrative:

Kemman niyahki tiankisko, niknekiyaya nimokowis se tamalli. Ipan noaltepetsin, monamaka tamalli tlen pitsonakatl. Pero amo nikpixki tomin, san pitsawak. Nikillia tlanamakaketl, "Keski ipatiw eyi tamalli?" wan nechillih, "Ompowalli wan mahtlakli pesoh." San nimokowih se, wan nokka nimayanayaya. Wankinon nikittak nowampoh Julio, wan nechillih "nimitstlanewtis ompowalli pesoh." Naman nitlawika tomin pero niyolpaktok.

Reduplication

Reduplication is a common feature of Nahuatl. In Classical Nahuatl, nouns could be reduplicated as a method of pluralization (konetl > kokoneh `children'). Verbs can also use reduplication, only the meaning isn't plural, but rather extends the meaning of the root verb, often by intensifying the verb or having the verb occur several times repeatedly. Sometimes the reduplication include an /h/, other times it will instead use a short or long vowel (not marked here). Reduplication of non-verbs tends to have a distributive meaning (every).

nemi
to be out and about

nehnemi
to walk

notsa
to call out to someone

nohnotsa
to call by phone

mawi
to fear s.t.

mahmawi
to fear s.t.

saka
to transport something

sasaka
to transport from many places

kwa
to eat something

kwahkwa
to chew on something

se
one

sehsen
each one

metstli
month

mehmetstli
every month

You'll also find synonyms with verbs that end in **-ni** in one form, and end in **-ka** with reduplication in a second form. They are especially common with verbs of sound or motion.

tomoni	`to sound like s.t. heavy fell'	**totomoka**
chipini	`to drip'	**chichipika**
kapani	`to sound like shoes or hooves'	**kakapaka**
kalani	`to sound like rattles'	**kakalaka**

19.

Verb Suffixes

Nahuatl makes use of many suffixes that attach directly onto a verbal root and change the meaning of the root. In a sense, these suffixes create completely new words and result in new separate entries in a dictionary. Though there are many suffixes, familiarizing yourself with these patterns will help you break down long words and better prepared to tackle new and unfamiliar sentences. Many suffixes overlap in meaning, and only practice and a handy dictionary can help you know which suffix to take.

Before reviewing all the suffixes, it's important to first practice and gain a basic understanding of their implications. Consider the word `run' in English. We can readily use this as an intransitive `I run'. We can also use it as a transitive `I ran him off'. We can do the same with `I walk' and `I walk my dog'. With few exemples, Nahuatl does not let a verb be both transitive and intransitive, it separate them into two distinct groups. This is where the verbal suffixes come in. Verbal suffixes may let us change an intransitive verb into a transitive verb, or at least add a new meaning to a transitive verb.

Let's pick the verb **kowa** `to buy something'. If I wanted to say `I'll buy you a tamal', you could not simply say:

> *Nimitskowa se tamal. *I'll buy you a tamal.

Kowa means `to buy something', so when one says **nimitskowa**, they are literally saying `I buy YOU', as if humans were being bought and sold. This distinction is a huge difference to how English works. The new verb we need is **kowia**, which we can visually tell is similar to **kowa**. **Kowia** means `to buy something for/from someone'.

> **Nimitskowia se tamal.** I'll buy a tamal for/from you.

Let's see another example with **namaka** `to sell something'. If I want to say `I sell you pants', I could not use the **namaka** form. Again, when I use **mits** (to you) with **namaka**, I am implying that I am buying YOU, since YOU are the object of **namaka** `to buy something'. The verb we want is **namakiltia** `to sell something to someone'.

> *Nimitsnamaka se pantalon. I sell you. One pant.

> **Nimitsnamakiltia se pantalon.** I sell pants to you.

Exercise 45 — Keniwki moillia?

1. I will buy a tortilla._____

2. I will buy you a tortilla._____

3. I sell clothes._____

4. I will sell you clothes._____

5. I cry. _____

6. You make me cry. _____

7. Money is lacking._____

8. I'm lacking money (money is lacking to me)._____

9. She comes out. _____

10. He takes her out (makes her come out)._____

11. You die. _____

12. I kill you (make you die). _____

miki	to die (ni)	**kisa**	to come out (ni)
miktia	to make someone die (nik)	**kixtia**	to take s.t. or s.o. out of something (nik)
poliwi	for something to be lacking, missing (ni)	**poloa**	for someone to be missing or lacking something (nech)
choka	to cry (ni)	**chokiltia**	to make someone cry (nik)
namaka	to sell something (nik)	**namakiltia**	to sell something to someone (nik)
kowa	to buy something (nik)	**kowia**	to buy something for someone (nik)

In this section you will gain an awareness of verb endings, but do not feel pressure to memorize them, rather, they are simply important to recognize.

In the change between **namaka** and **namakilia**, you may have noticed the only difference was the extra ending of **-ilia**. This is an example of verbal endings. There are two main types of verbal endings in Nahuatl, the causatives and applicatives, and some can be both.

Causatives	Either Causative or Applicative	Applicative
-a; -oa; -tia; -itia; -altia	-ltia; -wia; -lia	-ia; -wilia; -lilia

We can find many pairs of verbs distinguished by the causative **-a**, especially with intransitives that end in **-ni** and **-wi**. These are especially common with verbs that describe the actions of physical objects. Sometimes it deletes a weak /i/.

Intransitive	Transitive
kotoni something rips	**kotona** to rip something
kopini it becomes unstuck	**kopina** to unstick something
tlapowi it opens	**tlapoa** to open something
kalaki to enter	**kalakia** to make s.t. enter

Many roots ending in **-iwi** have a transitive pair with **-oa**.

Intransitive	Transitive
poliwi something is lacking	**poloa** for someone to lack something
kwesiwi to be bored	**kwesoa** for something to make you sad
apachiwi for a place to flood	**apachoa** to soak something in water

The study of verb endings in Huasteca Nahuatl was greatly furthered by the Nahuatl team at IDIEZ (Instituto de Docencia e Investigación Etnológica de Zacatecas).

-**tia** makes intransitive verbs from class 2 into transitives.

Intransitive	Transitive
mahmawi to be scared	**mahmawtia** to cause someone to be scared
mati to know	**machtia** to cause someone to know
paki to be happy	**paktia** to cause someone to be happy
nesi to appear	**nextia** to cause something to appear

-**itia** can be of any verb class. While similar to -**tia**, notice how -**itia** is always after a consonant, while the -**tia** of -**itia** ends in an -**i**.

Intransitive	Transitive
ahsi to reach, arrive	**ahxitia** to complete something
yoli to be alive	**yolitia** to cause something to live
ixwi to be full	**ixwitia** for something to cause indigestion in you, fill you up

Some verbs ending in -**ni** don't have a -**na** pair, but instead take -**altia**.

Intransitive	Transitive
patlani to fly	**patlanaltia** to make something fly
posoni for foam to appear	**posonaltia** to make foam appear
palani for something to rot	**palanaltia** to make something rot

We've seen causatives simply `cause someone or something to do X'. Applicatives don't make anyone do an action, but they do apply an action toward them. This is why Nahuatl has no specific word that means `for' or `from'. This meaning is given by verb endings. Consider the difference between these meanings in English.

Intransitive	Transitive	Causative	Applicative
I know.	I know it.	I cause you to know (teach you)	I let you know (applied knowledge to you)
I sell.	I sell it.	I make you sell.	I sell to you.
I ask.	I ask you.	I make you ask.	I ask of you, I ask from you.
I leave.	I leave you.	I make you leave it.	I leave it for you.

-ltia can be either a causative or (rarely) an applicative.

Base form	Causative	Applicative
mati to know s.t.	**matiltia** to make someone know	
oni to drink s.t.	**oniltia** to give someone a drink	
pano to pass	**panoltia** to make someone pass	
namaka to sell s.t.		**namakiltia** to sell s.t. to s.o.

-wia is a rare form only used with these three:

Base form	Causative	Applicative
saniloa to talk		**sanilwia** to talk with s.o.
illia to tell s.o. s.t.		**ilwia** to tell s.o. s.t. (synonymous with illia)
temo to get down	**temowia** to get something down	

-lia as a causative attaches to verbs ending in -wi, -wa, -ya, -ti, and -tiya. When added to -ya endings, it will delete the sequence /ya/.

Base form	Causative
tlatsiwi to be lazy	**tlatsiwilia** to make oneself feel lazy (nimo)
potewi to smell rotten	**potewilia** to let something smell rotten
miakiya to become plentiful	**miakilia** to cause something to become plentiful.
istlakati to lie	**istlakatilia** to lie to s.o
sentiya for a place to get filled with people (become one)	**sentilia** to get people together for a meeting

-lia takes on many verbs, giving them an applicative sense.

Base form	Applicative
tsintlayowa to get dark	**tsintlayowilia** to get dark for someone
wetska to laugh	**wetskilia** to laugh at someone
tsakwa to close s.t.	**tsakwilia** to close s.t. for s.o.
iskaltia to make s.t. grow	**iskaltilia** to make s.t. grow for s.o.
kawa to leave s.t.	**kawilia** to leave s.t. for s.o.
miktia to kill s.o.	**miktilia** to kill s.o. for s.o. else
neltoka to believe s.t.	**neltokilia** to believe s.t. from s.o.

-ia is an applicative that can delete the final vowel of a verb.

Base form	Applicative
palewi to help in general (not used)	**palewia** to help s.o.
pinawa to be shy, ashamed	**pinawia** to make s.o. shy, feel embarrassed.
tlachpana to sweep the floor	**tlachpania** to sweep the floor for yourself (nimo)
tlapehpena to pick things	**tlapehpenia** to pick things for yourself (nimo)
ateka to pour water	**atekia** to pour water on s.o. or s.t.

-wilia is an applicative that attaches to **-oa** ending verbs, but also deletes this sequence. It can also be used with **-lia** ending verbs, and verbs ending in **-tsa** (if they have reduplication).

Base form	Applicative
kweloa to bend s.t.	**kwelwilia** to bend s.t. for s.o.
siloa to dice s.t.	**silwilia** to dice s.t. for s.o.
patlachoa to flatten s.t.	**patlachwilia** to flatten s.t. for s.o.
tlalia to put or place s.t.	**tlalwilia** to put or place s.t. for s.o.
totomotsa to start s.t. with a loud engine	**totomotswilia** to start s.t. with a loud engine, for s.o.

Lastly we have the ending **-lilia,** only used with one verb.

Base form	Applicative
kwa to eat s.t.	**kwalilia** to eat s.t. that belongs to s.o. else

It is not necessary to memorize all the rules of all the verb endings in order to speak Nahuatl. One will gain familiarity through practice and exposure. The important lesson here is to gain the awareness of how these endings change the way you conjugate verbs, making the distinction between transitive and intransitive verbs, or adding two objects to a verb, thus requiring you to figure out which object prefix to use. An example is given below, where **kawa** takes /**k**/ as a prefix, since `book' is the object, and **kawilia** takes /**mits**/ as the object, since `you' is the object..

nikkawa amoxtli.   **Nimitskawilia se amoxtli.**

I leave a book.   I leave you a book/I leave a book for you.

Exercise 46 — Keniwki moillia?

1. I will eat you._____

2. I will eat your tortillas._____

3. I will make you eat tortillas._____

4. I work. _____

5. I employ it (I use it)._____

6. You take the *metate* out. _____

7. You take the *metate* from me._____

8. She tastes the food._____

9. She gives me food to taste. _____

kwa	to eat s.t.	tekiti	to work
kwaltia	to make s.o. eat food	tekiwia	to employ s.t.; utilize s.t.
kwalilia	to eat s.o.'s food	metlatl	metate
kixtia	to take s.t. out	machilia	to taste s.t.
kixtilia	to take s.t away from s.o.	machiltilia	to give s.o. food to taste

159

Vocabulary: Classroom

Welis nipanos?	May I go in?	**matlalana**	to raise one's hands. (nimo) (Class 2)
tlakaki	to listen, pay attention (ni) (Class 2).	**tlahtlanilistli**	a question
siawkawa	to rest (nimo) (Class 2)	**tlahtlania**	to ask a question (nik) (Class 3)
poliwi	for someone to be missing (ni) (Class 2)	**tlahtlanilia**	to ask s.o. a question (nik) (Class 3)
nikan niitstok	I'm here	**powa**	to count, read, retell s.t. (nik) (Class 2)
kwamachilia	to understand s.t. (nik) (Class 3)	**tlapoa**	to open s.t. (nik) (Class 3)
tlikolli	pen, pencil	**ihkwiloa**	to write, draw s.t. (nik) (Class 3)
tlahkwilolli	s.t. written	**ixpoloa/ ixpoliwiltia**	to erase s.t. (nik) (Class 3)
wapaltlahkwilolli	blackboard, whiteboard	**amoxtli/ amochtli**	book
nextia	to present s.t. (nik) (Class 3)	**wasania**	to scratch or scribble s.t. (nik) (Class 3)
nextilia	to present s.t. to s.o. (nik) (Class 3)	**tlatskiltia**	to stick or glue s.t. (nik) (Class 3)
piwia	to add s.t. (nik) (Class 3)	**kixtilia**	to remove, subtract from s.t. (nik) (Class 3)
piwilia	to add s.t. to s.t. else (nik) (Class 3)	**miakilia**	to multiply, increase s.t.
nehnewilia	to think about s.t. (nik) (Class 3)	**nehnemilia**	to think about s.t. (nik) (Class 3)
ilkawa	to forget s.t. (nik) (Class 2)	**ilnamiki**	to remember s.t. (nik) (Class 2)

Conversation

Tlamachtihketl: Piyali momachtianih, namantsin tipewaseh ika lenguaje, tlahtolmatilistli.

Lucas: (kochtok)

Tlamachtihketl: Eh, Lucas, xiihsa!

Lucas: Ah. Niihsatok san nitlanehnewilia!

Tlamachtihketl: Wakka xitlakaki. Momachtianih, xikitskikan inmoamox.

Tlamachtihketl: Lucas, tlen timomachtiseh?

Lucas: Nikilkawki.

Tlamachtihketl: Xikitski moamox tlen tlahtolmatilistli!

Lucas: Nikilkawki nochan...

Tlamachtihketl: Xiktlahtlanili se mowampoh ma mitsmakas.

Lucas: Dominga, welis xinechtlanewti amoxtli? Tlaskamati.

Lucas: Tlamachtihketl, ya nikpiya!

Tlamachtihketl: Xiktlapo amatl 144 wan xikpowa.

Lucas: Kena.... Axnesi tlahkwilolli. Se akahya kihkwiloh ipan amatl.

Tlamachtihketl: Nikan eltok se tlaixpoliwiltihketl. Xikixpolo.

Lucas: Tlaskamati.

Lucas: Tlanki.

Lucas: Kihtoa: Ipan xiwitl 1810 weyi altepetl Mexiko tlatlanki inon yaoyotl, inon netewilistli. Wankinon...

Dominga: Tlamachtihketl! Kenke motewiyaya?

Tlamachtihketl: Kwalli tlahtlanilistli Dominga. San, moneki ximomatlalana achtowi.

Dominga: Kena. Nikilkawki.

Tlamachtihketl: Wenoh, nimechpowilis kenke.

itskia	to grab s.t.	nesi	to appear
tlatlani	to win	netewilistli	a fight
moneki	it's necessary	powilia	to tell s.o. s.t., especially a story

20.

Miscellaneous Verb Patterns

While we've covered the major grammatical patterns of Huasteca Nahuatl, there's a few remaining patterns in verbs that will help you make new words and better understand other verbs.

Impersonal TLA

We've seen TLA before, but here we have a new meaning. This TLA takes a verb that has a subject and eliminates the subject. The verb **seseya** means `something gets cold'. When used, it will refer to a specific object like a cup, a bowl of soup, tortillas, etc. Placing the impersonal TLA will create the meaning `things get cold in general'. This TLA is used frequently to describe the weather, almost implying `it gets cold all over'. Lastly, TLA can be used with any verb, but if it's transitive it must already be satisfied.

seseya
it gets cold (specific)

tlaseseya
it's cold (the weather)

awetsi
it falls (water) (specific)

tlaawetsi
it's raining

totoniya
it gets warm (specific)

tlatotoniya
it's hot (the weather)

nesi
it appears (specific)

tlanesi
it's sunrise

yowa
it gets dark (specific)

tlayowa
it gets dark, nighttime

eltok
it's present (inanimate)

san tlaeltok
the weather is calm (it's just there)

tomoni
to sound like something heavy falling

tlatomoni
it thunders

petlani
it shines (specific)

tlapetlani
there's lightning

wetska
he laughs (specific)

tlawetska
there's laughter (in general at a place)

-TI, -YA and -TIYA

TI, YA and TIYA are endings that attach to nouns and turn it into a verb, sometimes meaning `it becomes X', or `it becomes like X'.

atl
water

atiya
it melts

kakistli
a sound

kakisti
it makes a sound (becomes literally)

montli
a man's Father-in-law

monti
to go live with one's father in law (due to marriage).

oktli
alcohol, fermented

oktiya
to become fermented

owih
difficult

owihti
to have difficulty, become difficult

kamatl
mouth

kamati
to speak (to use one's mouth)

-WI and -WIYA

WI and WIYA do the same as YA and TIYA.

setl
something cold

sewi
it becomes cold, turns off

kwawitl
tree

kwawi
to become stiff

*til
root meaning `thick'

tilawiya
to become thick

-IWI

The last major verbalizer is IWI.

atolli
a thick corn drink

atoliwi
to become thick

chilli
chili

chichiliwi
to become red

Exercise 47 — Complete the missing blanks.

sewetsi
ice falls

tlasewetsi
it's snowing/hailing (in general)

totonik
it's hot (specific)

it's hot (weather)

it sprinkles (specific)

tlapitsawkawetsi
it's sprinkling (weather)

achichipika
it drips (specific)

tlaeheka
it's windy (weather)

ayowi
fog exists

Exercise 48 — Keniwki moillia?

1. He will get big.

2. I will get fat.

3. It got lower.

4. I will not get any taller any more.

5. She will sturdy herself to pick something up.

weyi	big	**tomawak**	fat
weyiya	to get big	**tomawa**	to get fat
wahkapantik	tall	**echkapan**	short
wahkapantiya	to become tall	**echkapaniwi**	for s.t. to become lower (like a tree branch)
tetl	rock	**tetiya**	to become like a rock, strong, brace yourself
ayok	no longer		

164

Vocabulary: Time

kwalkan	morning	**kwalkanya**	3-5 am
tlahkotona	midday	**tlahkotonaya**	9-11 am
tiotlak	early evening	**tiotlakka**	2-6 pm
tlayowa	night	**tlayowaya**	evening
tlanesi	sunrise	**ixtsintlayowa**	it starts to get dark
tlahkoyowal	midnight	**yowatsinko**	morning (before sun rises)
tona	the sun shines; it's sunny	**metstona**	the moon shines
tlixiwitl	comet	**metstli**	moon
tonatiw	sun	**mixtli**	cloud
sitlalin	star	**tlamixtentok**	it's cloudy

In the traditional village setting, men and women begin work before the sun rises. This may be why the terms dealing with `midday' are much earlier in time than the English concept of midday.

You won't generally tell the time in Nahua villages, instead, the day is broken into periods based on the sun/moon's position. In situations where specific times are required, an ancient word meaning time, kawitl, has started to be used across many Nahuatl towns to mean `hour'.

se kawitl	one hour
ipan chikweyi kawitl	at 8 pm

21.

Variation in the Huasteca

The Huasteca holds the largest variety of Nahuatl in existence, likely composing of half of all Nahuatl speakers in this one region. However, there is also minor variation within the Huasteca. Research in the Huasteca variation exists from John Garcia (See: *Phylogenetic methods in Huasteca Nahuatl dialectology. by Garcia, John, M.A., California State University, Long Beach, 2014*). In this thesis, Garcia finds that Nahuatl speakers entered the Huasteca from the south-east near the valleys of Tulancingo. A relatively large split occurred as some Nahuatl speakers continued moving north, while another moved east. Most of the Huasteca was likely composed of Huastec (Tenek) communities. Tenek is a variety of Maya and Nahuatl borrowed several words from Tenek (**palach** = male turkey); (**kwapelech** = rooster). A few communities are bilingual in both, mostly in the state of San Luis Potosi.

Reference this map of the Huasteca. 1-5 are in the State of San Luis Potosi. 6-11, 17,18,20,21 are in Hidalgo. 16 is in Puebla. 12-15, 19, 22 are in Veracruz. Acaxochitlán is in Hidalgo but is actually a central variant with Huasteca similarities.

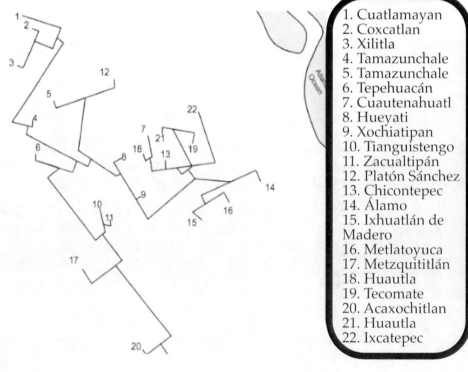

1. Cuatlamayan
2. Coxcatlan
3. Xilitla
4. Tamazunchale
5. Tamazunchale
6. Tepehuacán
7. Cuautenahuatl
8. Hueyati
9. Xochiatipan
10. Tianguistengo
11. Zacualtipán
12. Platón Sánchez
13. Chicontepec
14. Álamo
15. Ixhuatlán de Madero
16. Metlatoyuca
17. Metzquititlán
18. Huautla
19. Tecomate
20. Acaxochitlan
21. Huautla
22. Ixcatepec

Some words are different only by a vowel change. Reference the map to see which towns pronounce which form.

ehekatl `wind'	ahakatl `wind'
9, 10, 13-17, 19, 21, 22	1-8, 11, 12, 9, 18

tepasolli `nest'	tapasolli `nest'
1-4, 7-9, 12-13, 16, 18, 20-22	5- 9, 11, 19

wahkapantik `tall'	wehkapantik `tall'
9-12, 14-16, 18, 19	1, 3, 5, 7-9, 13, 17, 21-22

ilwikatl `sky'	elwikatl `sky'
23, 5, 9-11, 13, 16-17, 20	7, 12, 18, 19, 21

Some towns use different vocabulary forms

yayawik `black'	tliltik `black'
1-9, 12-16, 18-19, 21	2, 10, 11, 17, 20, 22

tlaawetsi `rains'	kiyawi `rains'
1,2, 9, 12-16, 18-19, 21,22	4, 6, 9-11, 17, 20

kwahtli `hawk'	kwatohtli `hawk'
1-3, 6, 9, 13, 16, 19, 21, 22	5, 7, 9-12, 17, 18

Some words have both vocabulary differences and sound differences.

naman `now, today'	aman `now, today'	axan `now, today'
6, 8-11, 14-17, 19, 21	1-5, 7, 12-13, 22	17, 20

Some words have a three way variation.

tsintamal 'butt'	tsintenno 'butt'	tsinpamitl 'butt'
2, 3, 7, 14, 16, 19, 21, 22	5, 8, 12, 14	1, 4, 10, 11, 13, 17

pepe 'toad'	tamasollin 'toad'	pechpechin 'toad'
1, 3	5, 6, 10-12	4, 9, 16, 19, 21, 22

The subregion of 5 and 12 have lost the /tl/ sound to /t/.

atl 'water'	at 'water'
all else	5, 12

Grammatically, some towns prefer **inihwantin** to mean 'they' and some prefer **yahwantin**. **Yahwantin** exists due to its similarity to **ya** 'he/she'.

inihwantin 'they'	yahwantin 'they'
3, 5, 7, 10-13, 20, 22	1,2, 4, 9, 14-17, 19, 21

A second grammatical distinction is between the subject pronouns **an-** 'you all' and **in-** 'you all'.

an- 'you all'	in- 'you all'
1-3, 6, 10, 12, 20	7-9, 14-16, 19, 21, 22

The word for 'cockroach' has a wide amount of variation.

kakarachi 'cockroach'	xopepe 'cockroach'	xopili 'cockroach'	xokotso 'cockroach'	kwapisi 'cockroach'
1-3, 5-6	7-10, 13-15, 17-19, 21,22	9, 12, 17	16	11

Possible words for the word 'squirrel' include: **tsokoro, tekomahtli, tokontsin, tekontsin, tsotsonkolli, tokomahtli and techalotl.**

Vocabulary: Fruits and Produce

alaxox	oranges	**kahtsotl**	jicama
chalchokotl	guayaba	**ilimon**	lemon
tsopelatl	fruit juice, soda	**mankoh**	mango
owatl	sugar cane	**kwatlakketl**	fruit
xipewa	to peel s.t. (nik) (class 2)	**tlaxintli**	sliced fruit
tsapotl	zapote fruit	**kokah**	annona
nochtli	prickly cactus pear	**xokonochtli**	sour cactus fruit
awakatl	avocado	**matsahtli**	pineapple
ipetlayo	it's rind, skin (fruit)	**kwaxilotl**	banana
kwalo	a spoiled or insect-bitten fruit	**ahwiyak**	delicious
tlaki	for a tree to grow fruit	**iwksi**	for fruit to ripen

Text about Fruits

Xikixmati kwatlakketl tlen tlaki ipan kwawitl. Se kwatlakketl tlen xoxoktik ayikana iwksitok. Moneki ximochiya wan ayikana xikteki inon kwatlakketl. Nohkiya xikmachili ipetlayo tlan chikawak so yamanik.

Nochi mochiwa ika atl: Alaxoxatl, ilimonatl, owaatl, mankohatl; so ika atolli: alaxoxatolli, eloatolli, sinatolli. Melawak ahwiyak nochi kwatlakketl.

169

22.

Cross Regional Comparisons

Now that we've seen variation within the Huasteca, we can compare the Huasteca to other regions. This section has the intent to better prepare the reader with the challenge of comprehending other regions. Examining all variation is outside the scope of this section, but we can cover the main differences.

`To be'

The verb `to be present' in the Huasteca is /**itstok**/ and /**eltok**/ for animates and inanimates, respectively. To exist, generally, is /**onkah**/. Central varieties tend to use a form of /**kah**/, which is irregular and changes to /**ye**/ in the future and command forms. Some modern towns use one or the other, or both.

Huasteca	Central
nikan niitstok `I'm here'	nikan nikah `I'm here'
nikan eltok se amoxtli `I'm here'	nikan kah se amoxtli `Here's a book'
nielis nitlamachtihketl `I will be a teacher'	niyes nitemachtianih `I will be a teacher'

Plurals

Almost all varieties use -meh for pluralizing animate nouns. Classical, Central and some towns in Guerrero use -tin.

Huasteca	Central
tlakameh `men'	**tlakatin** `men'
totolimeh `turkey hens'	**totoltin** `turkeys'

`Now'

Most Huasteca towns say `**aman**' or `**naman**', while Central tends toward `**axan**' or `**axkan**'.

Huasteca	Central
Aman/Naman	Axan/Axkan

`Next, More'

The word `ok' is generally used in Nahuatl varieties to mean `more, next, until'. However, the Huasteca tends to fuse this onto the end of adverbs.

Huasteca	Central
mostlayok `until tomorrow'	ok mostla `until tomorrow'
achiyok `a little more, more'	ok achi `a little more, more'
seyok `another one, next	ok se `another one, next'
sampa `again'	ok sepa `again'
sekinok `another person, other'	ok sekin `another person, other'

Reflexives

Recall from the reflexive section that Huasteca only uses **mo** as the reflexive, Guerrero only uses **no** as the reflexive, and Central varieties may make the ancient distinction between **no** (1st person singular), **to** (1st person plural) and **mo** (everyone else).

Huasteca	Central	Guerrero
nimoitta	ninotta	ninotta
moitta	motta	notta
timoittah	titottah	tinottah

Don't

Other varieties may use `maka' or `makamo' to negate a command, similar to `don't'.

Huasteca	Central
Amo xiyaw `don't go'	Makamo xiyaw `don't go'

`To come'

Central and other regions will use `wits' meaning `to come'. This verb had a related form `wallaw', which is now generally used in the Huasteca and several other regions.

Huasteca	Central
chokatiwallaw `she comes crying'	chokatiwits `she comes crying'
nopayoh wallaw `he's coming there'	ompa wits `he's coming there'

The Imperfect

Huasteca uses the form -yaya as the imperfect, while Central simply use -ya.

Huasteca	Central
wetskayaya `she was laughing'	wetskaya `she was laughing'
nechnotsayaya `he used to call me'	nechnotsaya `he used to call me'

`To say'

There's generally a four way distinction for the verb `to say'. Central says `tlahtoa'. Huasteca tends to say either saniloa/kamati/kamanalti. In the Huasteca, saying `tlahtoa' makes grammatical sense, but is generally unused, or it may imply speaking Spanish. The next common form is `tlapowi', used in the Sierra Negra/Orizaba/Zongolica regions around central Veracruz. A few towns (distant from each other) use the verb `tlaketsa', including Michoacan, Pipil Nawat, and at least one

Past Tense

Central varieties use the prefix o- to mark the past tense. This also results in Class 2 singular verbs not requiring a suffix.

Huasteca	Central
chokak `he cried'	ochokak `he cried'
pewki `it started'	opew `it started'

Much of the variation can be summed up as vocabulary differences.

Vocabulary	Huasteca	Central-based
eyes	-ixtiyol	-ixtelolo
delicious	ahwiyak	welik
nothing	axtlen	atlei
yes	kena	kema
a little	achi/kentsin	achi/tepitsin
or	so/o	noso/anoso
but	pero/sanpampa	pero/yese
this	inin/ni	inin/in
that	inon/ne/nopa	inon/on
no longer	ayokkana	aok
not yet	ayikana	ayamo
never	axkemman	aik
nowhere	axikah	ahkampa/ahkan
no one	axakah/amo akah	amo akin
all	nochi	mochi
when	kemman	kemman/ihkwak
why	kenke	tleika

Independent pronouns across all varieties may seem vastly different, but there is a clear pattern of change and simplification. Pronouns may be any of the following.

I, Me	nehwatl	nehwa/ nahwa	neha/ naha	neh / nah	ne / na
You	tehwatl	tehwa/ tahwa	teha / taha	teh / tah	te / ta
He, She, Him, Her	yehwatl	yehwa/ yahwa	yeha / yaha	yeh / yah	ye / ya
Us, We	tohwantin/ tehwantin	tehwan			
You all	inmohwantin/ anmohwantin	anmohwan			
They, Them	inihwantin/ yehwantin	yehwan			

The /h/ in ancient Nahuatl, Classical Nahuatl and some modern towns is pronounced as a glottal stop /'/. While this sound doesn't exist as a phoneme in English, it is similar to the stop in `uhohh'.

-Ya in Adverbs

One can find many similarities between Huasteca and Central varieties when we note the pattern that many adverbial-like words in Huasteca end in **-ya**.

Huasteca	Central
akahya `someone'	akah `someone'
akkiya `who?'	akin `who?'
kanahya `somewhere'	kanah `somewhere'
katlinya `which?'	katlin `which?'
iwanya `with'	iwan `with'
makaya `no, err i meant...'	maka `don't'
kemmanya `sometimes'	kemmaniyan `sometimes'
nopaya `over there'	ompa `over there'
nelliya `really, honest'	nelli `really, honest'
nowkiya `also'	noiwki `also'
wiptlaya `the day before yesterday'	wiptla `the day before yesterday'
yalwaya `yesterday'	yalwa `yesterday'

-Cha in Guerrero

A common sound change in Guerrero Nahuatl is for verbs ending in -**tia** to be changed to **-cha**. This also means the two syllables of -**tia** become one syllable in -**cha**, and thus the position of stress will change.

Huasteca	Guerrero
nimitstlaskamatilia `I thank you'	nimitstlasohkamacha `I thank you'
nimitstlakwaltia `I make you eat'	nimitstlakwalcha `I make you eat'

Reducing `tinech'

The sequence **tinech-** is made up of **ti** (the subject pronoun `you'), and **nech** (the object pronoun `to me'). For example: **tinechitta** `you see me', **tinechmiktis** `you will kill me', **tinechmakas** `you will give me'.

In several towns spread throughout the Nahuatl speaking areas, and including some regions of the Huasteca, this sequence can be simplified in relaxed speech to `tech', not to be confused with the object pronoun `tech'. Context should be enough to make it clear which is being used

Techmaka achi atl?
Can you give me some water?

Techitta?
Can you see me?

Reverential/Respect

Classical and Central varieties make/made much use of the reverential mode of verbs. This is essentially composed by changing one's speech, so that a verb takes on both the reflexive **mo** and one of the applicative/causative endings. This construction is possible in the Huasteca, though it's no longer used for the reverential.

Choka.
She cries.

Mochokilia.
She cries (with respect, literally, she cries herself).

Kipiya.
He has/guards it.

Kimopiyalia.
He guards it (with respect).

Tiktlalia.
You place it

Tikmotlalilia.
You place it (with respect).

Xikkowa.
Buy it!

Xikmokowiti.
Buy it (with respect, literally, make yourself buy it)!

Kineki
He wants it.

Kimonekiltia
He wants it (with respect).

-weli vs., -saso

You will find a common difference with the adverbial endings in that the Huasteca uses -**weli**, while Central based varieties tend toward **saso**. These endings are similar to `-**ever**' in English.

Huasteca	Central
akkiyaweli `whoever'	saso akin `whoever'
kampaweli `wherever'	saso kampa `wherever'
kemmanweli `whenever'	saso kemman `whenever'
kenweli `however, in any way'	saso kenami `however, in any way'
tlenweli `whatever, any thing'	saso tlein `whatever, any thing'

Different Meaning

A few similar looking words have different meanings in different regions.

Huasteca	Central	Guerrero
niman `soon'	niman `and then'	niman `and'
teksistli `egg'	teksistli `large seashell'	
tekwani `wild animal'	tekwani `animal that eats humans'	tekwane `jaguar'

Double /L/ in Guerrero

The double /L/ in nouns in Guerrero is pronounced with the first L aspirated. Thus, you may see **kalli** written as **kahli** or **kajli**.

Nouns Ending in -i change to -e

The original ending of -**lli, -tli, -in** was likely the /i/ sound, but many central varieties have relaxed this sound to an /e/, thus producing words like **tlaxkalle, tamalle, tonalle**.

Comparison of Sentences

Below is the comparison of similar sentences in several different
Nahuatl towns across Mexico. These example sentences are adapted
from the website Bible.IS. The verse is John 21:10. See the vocabulary
below to help you spot the differences.

Western Huasteca	Wan techilwih: —Techwallikilikan se ome michimeh katlin ankinitskihkeh.
Eastern Huasteca	Wan techilwih: —Xinechwallikilikan se ome michimeh tlen inkinitskihkeh
Guerrero	Jesús okimihlih:—Xkinwalwikakan sekimeh michimeh yehwan kemach onenkimahsikeh.
Sierra Negra	Jesús okinmilwih:—Xikinvalikakan sekimeh michimeh tlen yikin onkoninkitskihkeh.
Sierra Norte, Puebla	Wan ihkón in Jesús quinilliaya ihkwín: —Xikwalkwikan sekin namopescados ten yekin nankinwalkwikkeh.
South East Puebla	Jesús okimillih: —Xikkwalinwikakan sikimeh michimeh non sikin ononkinkixtihkeh.
North Puebla	Wan Jesús okinilwilok: —Xikwallikakan sekin michtin in tlen welok nankikixtiyahkeh.
North Oaxaca	Jesús okimilwih: —Xikkwalinkwikan sekimeh michimeh katlen yakin ankinkitskihkeh
Michoacan	Jesús kimillik: Xikinwalikakan sekin michimes wal anlamik ankinkitskik.

ilwia/illia	to tell s.o. s.t.	**kin-/kim-**	to them
wallika/ walwika/ walinwika	to bring s.t.	**wallikilia/ walwikilia**	to bring s.t. to s.o.
se ome/ sekin	some	**michin**	fish
katlin/katlen	which	**itskia/kitskia**	to catch s.t.
an-/en-/in-/ non-	you all (prefix)	**kixtia**	to take s.t. out
tlami/lami	to finish	**yakin/ yekin/ welok**	just recently

177

Vocabulary: Taste

ahwiyak	delicious	**axahwiyak**	not delicious
poyek	salty	**tsopelik**	sweet
kokok	spicy	**xokok**	sour
poyeya	it becomes salty	**chichik**	bitter
kokoya	it becomes spicy	**tsopeliya**	it becomes sweet
machilia	to feel, taste s.t.	**xokoya**	it becomes sour
yehyekoa	to try s.t.	**amati**	to like s.t.
tlakwalli	prepared food	**tlakwalistli**	anything edible
sesek	cold	**totonik**	hot
ahwiyaka	s.t.'s deliciousness	**totoniya**	it becomes hot
istatl	salt	**newktli**	honey

Vocabulary: Kitchen

tlakwalchiwa	to prepare food (ni) (class 2)	**teki**	to cut s.t. (nik) (class 2)
tamalchiwa	to make tamales (ni) (class 2)	**xima**	to peel fruit with a knife (nik) (class 2)
tlaxkalchiwa	to make tortillas (ni) (class 2)	**atolchiwa**	to make atole (ni) (class 2)
mana	to place s.t. on the fire to cook (nik) (class 2)	**tlalia**	to place s.t. somewhere (nik) (class 3)
tekilia	to pour s.o. liquid (nik) (class 3)	**tekia/teka**	to pour liquid onto a cup (nik) (class 3/1)
tisi	to grind, to grind s.t. (ni) [or] (nik)	**moloni**	for water to boil (class 2)
tsoyonia	to fry s.t. (nik) (class 3)	**molonia**	to make s.t. boil (nik) (class 3)
pahpaka	to wash s.t. (except clothes) (nik) (class 1)	**paka**	to wash a specific piece of clothing (nik)(class 1)
nakatl	meat	**tixtli**	dough

Match, then place the answers on the crossword

(1) Tlawel sokiyoh inin polatoh. Nikneki _____.

(2) Tlawel sesek, poyek wan axahwiyak ni tlaxkalli, yeka amo _____.

(3) Nikmana kafen ipan tlitl pampa nikneki ma _____.

(4) Nikneki nikkwas etlatsoyontli. Nikpiya etl, naman _____.

(5) Monica amiki. Kineki ma _____ atl.

(6) Ipan ne atolli niktlalih miak newktli wan naman _____.

(7) Inin tlakwalli tlawel poyek pampa niktlalih miak istatl wan _____.

(8) Xikmachili ni tlakwalli wan xinechilli tlan sesek so _____.

Word Bank		
niktsoyonis	nikpahpakas	moloni
totonik	nikamati	niktekili
poyexki	tsopelik	

Tlakwalistli

Reading Nahuatl

Review the section on Nahuatl pronunciation at the beginning of this book. It is important to remember there are three main systems used to write Nahuatl, including the Classical Based-ACK system, the modern INALI system (used here) and the 20th century based S.E.P. (Mexican Education Department) system. Despite the popularity of all three systems, untrained speakers will write using their knowledge of Spanish writing conventions, written here as (Common).

Translation: We will sleep.
Modern: Tikochiseh.
S.E.P.: Tikochise.
ACK: Ticochizceh.
Common: Ti cochize.

Translation: I want to eat already since I'm already going to sleep.
Modern: Nikneki nitlakwassa pampa nikochissa.
S.E.P.: Nijneki nitlakuasa pampa nikochisa.
ACK: Nicnequi nitlacuazza pampa nicochizza.
Common: Nij nequi ni tlakwa sa pampa ni kochi sa.

Translation: Juan eats because he's hungry.
Modern: Juan tlakwa pampa mayantok.
S.E.P.: Juan tlakua pampa mayantok.
ACK: Juan tlacua pampa mayantoc.
Common: Juan tlacoa pampa mayan tuk.

Translation: If you hide in the forest you could get lost.
Modern: Tlan timotlatis ipan kwatitlan, welis timokwapolos.
S.E.P.: Tla timotlatis ipan kuatitlan, uelis timokuapolos.
ACK: Tlan timotlatiz ipan cuatitlan, hueliz timocuapoloz.
Common: Tlah ti mo tlatiz ipa cuatitlan, guelis ti mo koapolos.

Translation: The sun is coming soon.
Modern: Nimantsin wallaw tonatiw.
S.E.P.: Nimantsin uala tonatij.
ACK: Nimantzin huallauh tonatiuh.
Common: niman tsin goala tonati.

Translation:
Modern: Se wewetsin axwahka nechillamiki.
S.E.P.: Se ueuetsin axuajka nechilamiki.
ACK: Ce huehuetzin axhuahca nechillamiqui.
Common: Se gueguetcin ax uajca nech ilamiki.

Translation: Be well my friends on this night
Modern: Kwalli xiitstokan nowampoyowan ni tlayowa.
S.E.P.: Kuali xiitstoka nowampoyowa ni tlayoua.
ACK: Cualli xiitztocan nohuampoyohuan ni tlayohua.
Common: Cuali xi itztoca no mazehual pollohua nitlayow.

Some common patterns you may have noticed is confusion by native speakers of the difference between the letters /ll/ in Spanish and /y/. /ll/ for the sound [y] should only exist in Spanish, as it's a representation of an ancient Spanish sound that was something similar to [ly]. Nahuatl only needs /y/, and the spelling of /ll/ is to represent two actual /l/ next to each other.

     caballo, `horse' was pronounced [**kabalyo**] in ancient Spanish.

Secondly, one may not even know of the existence of /ll/ combinations in Nahuatl (tonalli, cualli, tlalli etc.), unless one studied it. This is because many towns don't hear a difference between two /l/ together.

Similar to this issue, is the fact that word final /n/ can be quite soft in spoken Nahuatl, especially in the Huasteca. However, writing it not only pays tribute to ancient Nahuatl, it also brings the system more united with other regions that continue to pronounce the /n/. Furthermore, the /n/ is like a ghost, it seems to be invisible, but can appear with the addition of another suffix.

     kafen (sounds like kafeh) --> **kafentik** (sounds like kafentik)
     ximoketsakan (sounds like ximoketsakah)
     nowampoyowan (sounds like nowampoyowah)

Nahuatl combines the subject and object prefixes onto the verb, but Spanish works entirely different, and it can appear that the subjects and objects are separate words. This is why the common writing system may separate words.

     nimitsitta (could be mistakenly written as ni mits itta)

SEP uses a /u/ to represent the /w/ sound. They are both actually pronounced the same, but /w/ better represents the fact that it's a consonant, not a vowel in Nahuatl. There was likely some resistance to adopting /w/ since it's considered to be an English letter.

You may see /j/ used instead of /h/, since /j/ is used in Spanish and /h/ is more common in English. Keep in mind, the /h/ sound in Nahuatl is a soft aspiration more similar to English than to the harsher /j/ sound of Spanish.

23.

Reading Texts

In this chapter you will get to apply all of the concepts we have covered thus far. Included here are short stories and songs in Huasteca Nahuatl, as well as a text from a Central-based variety. Some will contain a gloss and a translation, some will contain a translation only so you can try to break down the meanings, others will have none, in which case you'll have to rely on the dictionary at the end of this book.

Huasteca Song:
Monanan Motatah Chokah

Monanan, motatah chokah   pampa ta   timonamiktiya
your.mom your.dad they.cry because you already.getting.married
'Your mom and dad are crying because you're getting married.'

Xikilli axkanah ma choka pampa axkanah timiquitiyaw
tell.her not   to cry   because not   you.dying
'Tell her not to cry because you aren't dying.'

Tokomaleh   wan tokompaleh xikonikanya se winohtsin
our.co-mother and co-father   drink.already a alcohol
'Our friends, have some tequila/mezcal already.'

Wan axkanah kampeka mostla, wiptla innentiyaseh ika se kwesolli
and not   ceremony tomorrow, day-after ya'll.will.be with a
sadness
'And the ceremony's not tomorrow, the day after ya'll will be with sadness.'

Siwapil kemman tlanesi   xikmanaya se kafentsin
girl   when   it.dawns place!   a coffee
'Young girl, when dawn breaks get the coffee ready.'

Mowewe   yas   tequititi xikmakaya se tlaxkaltsin
your.husband going to.work give.him   a tortilla
'Your husband's going to work, give him his food already.'

Tokomaleh wan tokompaleh ya ni ika   timomakawaseh
our.co-mother and our.co-father (with this) will.let.ourselves.go
'Friends, with this we'll let ourselves go, we'll finish off.'

Inkionikehya   se tsopelik   astah mostlatsin tokompaleh
you.all.drank.already a refreshment until tomorrow our.co-father
'You all drank your refreshments, so until tomorrow friends.'

182

Huasteca Song:
Aman kena

Na nikpixtok se nochichi, wan nelkwalkan nelnikewa.
I have.had a dog and very.early I.get.him.up
  `I have a dog, and I get him up very early.'
Kiwaltoka nopa masatl wan nelliya kwalli tlatewa.
He.chased that deer and really well surprises
  `He chased the deer and is good at surprising.'
Aman kena, aman kena, aman kena tokomaleh.
now yes now yes now yes our.co-mother
  `Now's the time, now's the time, now's the time ma'am.'
Ya xiktlamaka nochichi ya xikmaka se tlaxkalli.
now feed my.dog now give.him a tortilla
  `Now feed my dog and give him a tortilla'.

Nochichi tlaahwayaya, kipantito tlakwakilotl,
my.dog was.barking he.went.to.find opossum
  `My dog was barking, he went to find the opossum.'
Kipantito tlakwayaya, kikwayaya millah xilotl.
he.went.to.find was.eating, was.eating field tender.corn
  `He went to find him eating, he was eating the field's corn.'
Aman kena, aman kena, aman kena tokomaleh.
now yes now yes now yes our.co-mother
  `Now's the time, now's the time, now's the time ma'am.'
Ya xiktlamaka nochichi ya xikmaka se tlaxkalli.
now feed my.dog now give.him a tortilla
  `Now feed my dog and give him a tortilla'.

Nochichi mosisinia, kitlankechih se ichpokatl,
my.dog gets.mad he.bit a girl
  `My dog gets mad, he bit a girl'
Kitlankechih itsintenno kitlankechih wanya itsonkal.
he.bit.her her.behind he.bit.her with her.hair
  `He bit her butt and her hair.'
Aman kena, aman kena, aman kena tokomaleh.
now yes now yes now yes our.co-mother
  `Now's the time, now's the time, now's the time ma'am.'
Ya xiktlamaka nochichi ya xikmaka se tlaxkalli.
now feed my.dog now give.him a tortilla
  `Now feed my dog and give him a tortilla'.

Koyochichi wan Koyotl

Se weltah eliyaya   se koyotlakatl   tlanamakaketl
one time   exist.used.to   one non.native.man seller
      `Once there was a non-native vendor.'

wan tlawel tekahkayawayaya.
and very   deceive.people.used.to
      `And he deceived a lot of people'

Axakah weliyaya   kikahkayawas.
no.one   able.used.to   deceive.him.future
      `No one could deceive him'

San se tonatiw, killih   se tlakatl
just one day   told.him   one man
      `Just on one occasion, a man told him"

"onkah se akahya   tlen welis   kena mitskahkayawas."
exists   one someone that   maybe   yes   will.deceive.you
      `There is someone who perhaps could trick you.'

Koyotlakatl killih   "nopa   axweli,
non.native   told.him   that not.possible
      `The non-native told him, "that's not possible'

nikinnamakakiltihtok masewalmeh miak xiwitl."
I.have.sold.to.them   people   many years
      `I've been selling to the natives for many years"'

Kinankillih   "Axkeniwki, ne koyochichi weli mitstlanis."
responded.to.him   no.matter   that   coyote   can   win.you
      `He responded, "Doesn't matter, that coyote can beat you."'

"Wankinon tikittaseh. Kanin itstok   Koyochichi?"
  thus   we.will.see where be.present coyote
      `Well, we'll see. Where is the coyote?

"Nepa   itstok." Wankinon ne Tlanamakaketl kinechkawih.
over.there   be.present then   that vendor   approached.him
      `"He's over there." Then the vendor approached him.

"Nikneki nikittas tlan tiwelis   tinechkahkayawas"
I.want   I.will.see if you.can you.deceive.me
      `I want to see if you can trick me."

Xinechtlapohpolwi, niknekiskia   nimitspalewiskia,
forgive.me   i.would.want i.help.you
    `"Sorry, I'd like to help you'

sanpampa nechpoloa   pahtli." "Pahtli? hahaha, xikonwallika."
but   to.me.lacking medicine medicine haha bring.it
    `but I'm missing medicine." "Medicine? haha. Bring it!"

Kinankilih   koyochichi
responded.to.him   coyote
    `The coyote responded to him.'

"Tlawel wahka nochan   wan san   ninehnentinemi.
very   far   my.house and just I.be.walking.place.to.place
    `"My house is very far and I'm just walking place to place.'

Moneki   nimitstlanewilis mokawayoh pampa chikawak motlaloa."
its.necessary i.borrow.from.you your.horse because fast   he.runs
    `I have to borrow your horse because he runs fast."'

"Kwaltitok. Ximokwapa mochan   wan nikonwallika pahtli."
good   return!   your.house and i.bring   medicine
    "Fine. Go back home and bring your medicine!"

Kiihtoh aporaroh.
he.said hurredly
    `He said in a hurry'.

"Nowanpoh, amo nikmati ken   ninemis ipan kawayoh.
my.friend no i.know.it how i.be   on   horse
    "My friend, I don't know how to ride a horse."

Nowkiya nechmawilia wan nikmawilia.
also   he.fear.me   and i.fear.him
    `also, he's scared of me and I'm scared of him.'

Xinechmaka moyoyon   se tlatoktsin,
give.me   your.clothes one moment
    'give me your clothes for a bit."'

iwkinin mokawayoh moillis   nielis ta" kiihtoh koyochichi.
like.this your.horse tells.himself i.be you said   coyote
    `this way your horse will think that I am you."*

"Kwaltitok, nikan eltok. Naman xiyaw xikonwallikati pahtli.
good   here be   now   go!   bring!   medicine
    "Fine, here it is, now go get the medicine!"

Nikmati niwelis nimitstlanis!"
i.know   i.can   i.beat.you
    `*I know I can beat you!"'*

Wankinon ne koyotl choloh ika iyoyon   wan ika ikawayoh,
then   that coyote fled with his.clothes and with his.horse
    `*Then the coyote ran away with his clothes and horse'*

** noke ne Koyotlakatl   mokawki   ihkatok wan xolotik.**
while that non.native left.himself   standing and nude
    `*While the non-native was left standing nude.'*

-Lakota humor story translated into Nahuatl. Original story told at Grass Mountain, Rosebud Indian Reservation, South Dakota, 1974. From American Indian Myths and Legends, Richard Erdoes and Alfonso Ortiz, 1984.

Huasteca Story:
Tsopilotl wanya ne Ostotl

Ne tsopilotl wanya ne ostotl.
Killia ne tsopilotl `uta'.
`Kwalli titlakwa tsopilotl.'
`Yehyektsin ta titlakwa.'
`Kena na kwalli ni tlakwa.'
`Pero na nipano puro tekitl.'
`Puro ne kwatitlan niitstok.'
Ostotl ya kihtoa ya axkwalli tlakwa.
Tsopilotl kwalli tlakwa pampa tlan miki se animal, ya kikwa.
`Makwa tlan tikneki no xiyaw.'
`Ma tiyakan titlatemotih tlen titlakwaseh.'
`Pero keniwki niyas wan axnikpiya noeltlapal.'
Wan killia, `Xitlatski ni nokwitlapan.'
`Wan tiyaseh titlatemotih tlen titlakwaseh.'
Ostotl, tlatskitoya ne ikwitlapan.
Ne kwitlapan tsopilotl.
Patlankiya tsopilotl yawiya.
Tlachiya iwkinin tlan axtlen wetstok se animal para tlakwaseh.
Mas tlehko mas tlehko mas wahkapan yowih.
Wahkapan ya yawki.
Tlachiya para kanin miktok se animal.
Se toro se burro se kawayoh.
Wan kitl mas tlehko tsopilotl.
Keni mochiwa, keni mochiwa, tlamaahki nopa ostotl.
Tlatsintlan wetsiko miktok.
Nopa tlanke mayanayaya. Mikki ostotl.

tsopilotl	turkey vulture	**miki**	to die (ni) (class 2)
ostotl	fox	**makwa**	well then...
uta	dang, wow	**tlatemoa**	to look for stuff
yehyektsin	pretty, very nice	**eltlapalli**	wings
pano	to pass, experience	**itskia**	to grab, hold onto, catch
kwatitlan	forest	**kwitlapan**	someone's back
patlani	to fly (ni) (class 2)	**tlachiya**	to observe (ni) (class 2)
wetsi	to fall down	**tlehko**	to climb up
wahkapan	up, high	**kitl, kil**	supposedly
tlatsintlan	down below	**tlamaahki**	to swing arms like swimming

Huastec Narrative.
A Nahua man tells us an experiences.

Se weltah tiahsitoskiah pan se tonel nopayo nechkatsin.
`One time we reached a tunnel there close by'

Pero axkanah tikalakkeh porque itstokeh nopa newkmeh tlen tekwah.
`But we didn't go in because there were those bees that sting'

Entonces, axkanah welki tipanoh nopayo kampa tohwantin timodetenerohkeh.
`So then we weren't able to pass there where we got stuck.'

Timokwapkeh sampa para tikkixtisehya fotografias.
`We returned again so we could take photographs.'

Pero axkanah neski yehyektsin nopa retratos.
`But they didn't appear well.'

Wan tiplanearohkeh kemmaniwki sampa tiyaseh, pero ayokkemman tiyawkeh.'
`And we planned when we could again go, but we never went.'

Nikan pan ni tepemeh, miak tlamantli onkah.
`In these hills, there's many things.'

Miak tlamantli tlen ta axkanah timoimaginaros,
`Many objects you wouldn't imagine.'

pero nikan poliwi se gobernador algo
`But here we need a governor or something.'

para kiinvestigaroskia kimandaroskia antropologos profesionales
`So he could investigate, send professional anthropologists.'

wan pan ni tocomunidad eliskia historia mas grande,
`And in our community there could be a bigger history.'

nochi piedras tlen tikahsih tikreuniskia moregistraroskia
`All the stones that we find we could reunite, register them.'

mokawaskia pan ni tokomunidad. pero de nopa axakah mopreocuparoa
`They could stay in our community. But no one cares about that.'

pero tlan mopreocuparoskia se akahya wan nemiskia welis kena.
`But if someone cared and he lived, maybe it could be done.'

Huasteca Narrative.
A Nahua man tells a story of demons/tricksters.

Elki se tlakatl axkanah kipiyaya tomin, se campesino pues.

San tlapalewiyaya nowkiya komo tohwantin.

Wan entonces, kimelawki se señor wan kilki tlan kineki tomin,

ya kipalewis, ma yowi pan ichan. Yawki pan ichan.

Yawki kiwikak pan ikabayo pero killia ma ihkopi.

Wan kemman ihkopki, tlachixtewki itstokeh ichan pan se tonel weyi,

kalihtik. Killia "ximosewi pan ne mokwasiyah."

Ya se koatl, se serpiente weyi, wan kiilia nopaya ma mosewi.

Apenas mosewiyaya, kinekiyaya kikwas.

Wan killia axkanah ma kimawili, porque tlan kimawilis kikwas.

Mosewih wan axkanah tlen kisusederoh, kimakak miak tomin

pero era Diablo, Diablo nopa persona.

Axkanah ya persona komo tohwantin.

Kipalewih nopa persona, kipixki miak tomin.

Kiilki san kipalewis pan chikome xiwitl.

Kiilki kipalewis, san kipalewiseh nopa diablo.

Wan kitlamilih kitlanewkeh wan kemman ahsiyaya chikome años,

ya kalakki kioraroa dios para axkanah kinekki yas

kipalewiti nopa Diablo. Wan kemman ahsitiyowiyaya chikome

años, este, wallawkeh ikonewan nopa Diablo.

Primero walki se tlen mas mayor.

Kiillia para, kinotsa itata ma kipalewiltiya.

Wan killia axkanah, ma mosewi.

Namantsin tikonitewas se tasa de kafén, wan namantsin tiyasseh.

Mosewih pan se kwasiya para kionis se kafé. Tlami kioni kafe.

Tlakwahkeh kikwahkeh se pan , naman kena vamos.

Kemman yowiyahya nopa Diablo tlen mayor, tlatskihki pan

nopa kwasiya. Tlatskih wan killia para kalakki tsatsi.

Killia para, "Axkanah xitsahtsi."

Nimitskopewilis nopa kwasiyah.

Motata nechkahkayawati. Axkanah tiixmelawtik.

Weno kena pues xikkopewa keniwki tikmati ta tikchiwas.

Porke nikmachilia para na nowkiya niyas.

Porke nechillihkeh san ma nionahsiki.

Kikopewilihki kichiwki se orasion.

Walahki seyok Diablo tlen menor.

Killia para, axkanah temo pan ikaballo ken ne ihkawtok.

Killia para kinotsa itata ma yowi nopa señor.

Wan killia para axkanah yas porke, pues ma temo.

"Axkanah xikwika miak prisa, xitemo."

"Axkanah ximoapuparo, namantsin titlakwasseh wan tiyasseh."

"Axkanah ximoapuparo, namantsin tiyasseh."

Wan este temok. "Ximosewi namantsin tiyaseh."

"Namantsin ma tikwallika se botana titlakwasseh."

Mosewih, tlakwahkeh, wan kemman kiillia,

"naman kena vamos, tlan xiknotsa mopapa."

Nowkiya pasaroh lo mismo, tlatskih pan kwasiya.

Wan kalakki tsahtsi, kalakki moawitaroa. killia para

kitsinkokoa nopa kwasiya por ke , tlatskitok nalga.

Wan killia, "Xikkopewa."

Kena pues, kalakki oraroa oraroa nopa tlakatl.

Nopa kwasiyah kopewki.

Wan keman kopewki, nopa muchacho yawki.

Tonilito wallawto mero inintata, mero ininpapa.

Mero Diablo el padre. Mero ya wallawki, killia, kiilki

kinotsako ikompa para ma kipalewiltiya porque

ne kichixtok chikome xiwitl. Wan kiillia para,

"Kena tiyasseh namantsin pero xikkwa se lalaxox.

porke miak lalaxox onkah san ika tlen tikkwaltlalih.

xikwatewa se lalaxox".

Axkinekiyaya kikwas, pero como itstihka,

killia kena kikwas se naranja.

Apenas kikwik nopa naranja—mopegarokeh, pan nopa iresina.

Nopa naranja tlatskih imah.

Wan killia para kalakki tsatsi nowkiya.

Killia para kenke imah tlatski nopa naranja.

"Nikneki xikkopewa nopa mero señor," killihkeh diablo, tlen mero padre.

Killia "na niktlalia axkanah kwakwalli.

Na niktlalia axkanah kwakwalli tinechtlalia ne tomin.

Melawak kineki techtraisionaros."

Wan nochi yeka— Kennopa nelli

axkanah kwakwalli inkisaseh ni mochan wan naman

xikkopewili. — Kena kopewas pero axkanah mitspalewis,

San ma tlami nopa trabajo.

Weno kena pues xikkopewa wan axkanah techpalewis.

San iwkinon ma tlamiya xiktekiwi nopa tlaxtlawilli tlen mitstenewtih.

Wan kichiwki se orasion, kopewki nopa imah.

entonses kalakki mokokoa mokokoa, mikki.

Wan yahki ne wahkapan, axkanah kipanoyaya dios pan nopa puerta.

Killia para ya kiseguiroa diablo, ma kiseguiro ya,

porque ya axkanah kipanoltiyaya nopa lugar,

porque ya tlatskihto weyi diablo.

Adaptation of Poem by Natalio Hernández Xocoyotzin

Nimitswikatis Masewalichpokatl

Nimitswikatis siwatl ichpokatl.
Xikseli ika moyollo ni tlatsotsontli tlen
Mitswikilia se masewaltelpokatl.

Yehyektzin telpokatl tiichpokanesi.
Miak liston ika mokwailpia.
siltik kostilli timocostia.
Ika pamitl timocuateposhuia.

Niyolpaki wan niyoltomoni.
kemman titetik tikonkwi atl.
Nohkiya kemman tiyaw tiankis.
Timokwapa ika wetskilistli.

Nikamati miak nimitstlakakilis.
kemman tiktlalia xochimeh pan motsontekon.
Nimitsmaktilis xochitl atl.
Ika xochitl atl ximokwailpi yehyektsin.

Tlawel nikamati mokechtlan.
Miak tlamantli nesi pan mopan.
Nopayo eltok tlallamikilistli tlen tototatahwan.
Tlallamikilistli tlen tiktlepanittas.
Wan tikahkokwis.

Nikamati san moixneska tlakayo.
Pampa tlatlawak tonana tlaltipaktli.
axkemman xikpinawi.
pampa quennopa tiahsiko pan ni nemilistli tlaltepaktli.

Letter Written by Emiliano Zapata

(He spoke a Central-based variety in Morelos)

An jefes, oficiales huan soldado de la division Arenas:

_____

Tlen tonochtin otikchiyaya yo tikittakeh.

_____

Axkan, yehwa non omochiwaskia axkan noso mostla de nan

_____

moxeloskia de nekate non akihque

_____

kitlakachiwan in Venustiano Carranza.

_____

Yehwan aik nanmechmapalewihkeh.

_____

Ni an aik nan wel tiktlasohtlakeh.

_____

Iwan kema nanmechtlalilihkeh miak nekahkayawalistli

_____

wan miak nexikoalistli ika non kwalli nankittakeh

_____

de que amo nanmechtlakapowkeh.

_____

Kinequiyah kikokoskeh nanmomawisolos.

_____

Wan nanmechtlahtlaksaskeh nonkes aik

---

nanmechittitihkeh nepechteka okichmatilistli.

Non aik mochiya de necate oquichtin tlen kahsihkamati.

San de tekotlasohtlalistli wan de nepechtekalistli tlanekilistikayopa,

---

wan de netlakamatilistli, itlaka tlampa

---

ipan tlen tewaxka wan itech akin tekitl kichiwa.

Non neixkwepaloni ipan amokwalli tlahtoani nanmawisyotia

---

wan kitlipoloa neka ilnamikilistli de nanmotlahtlakol.

Tehwani tlen tikikxichiya man tlatlani ipewaloni

---

netewilistli wan nesetilistli de tonochtin,

---

timotewianimeh itlampa se bandera.

Wan ihkon moweyichiwas non neyollosetilistli

---

tlen aik kitlaniskeh nonkes teka mokayawkeh.

Wan nochtin akihkeh kinmikawia non kitlakachiwah Carrancismo;

Tewantin ika nochi toyollo tikmatiilkawaskeh

nan yewahka nexikoalistli.

Tanmechyolewa nanmonochtin iwan akin kinekis

de namehwan nanmopowaskeh itlampa tobandera,

ka wel yehwa iwaxka in altepetl iwan tonawak nantekitiskeh

ipampa nesetil netewialoni, yehwan nan axkan iwan axkan

in ok achi weyi tekitl tlen tikchiwaskeh

ixpan totlaltikpaknantsin, mihtoa patria.

Man tiktewikan neka amo kwalli okichtli, Carranza,

tonochtin wel yewatl, totekokokayo.

Man timopalewikan tosepan tlampa

iwan ihkon tiktlaniskeh neka weyi tlanawatille

ipewaloni tlalle, libertad iwan justicia.

Man tikkumplirokan toteki de netewiloanimeh mawistikeh

---

iwan kimatih tlen kichiwaskeh.

Nan, tlen weyi iwan tlen tlaltikpaktlasohnantsin,

---

nanmechyolewa nin cuartel general den Ejercito libertador.

Ika non nikchiwa nin tlahtoltlanawatilistli,

Iwan nochi nekate akihkeh kitskiskeh tonetewilis, yewatl man ye

---

akin saso kipahpakilispiyas weli, wan melawak kwalli inemilis

---

Itech inin yawi tomawistikatlahtol,

---

de kwalli okichtin iwan de kwalli netewiloanimeh.

Reforma, libertad, justicia y ley.

Cuartel general

Tlaltizapan, Mor. a 27 de abril de 1918

El General en Jefe del Ejercito Libertador.

Common affixes in Morelos Nahuatl:

nan-	you all (subject prefix)	**-nimeh**	plural agentive suffix
nanmech-	you all (object prefix)	**te-**	non-specific object prefix (to people in general)
nanmo-	your (2nd person plural possessive prefix)	**-ya**	imperfect tense (-yaya in Huasteca)

The rest of the word bank below:

an	to those who (a combination of Spanish /a/ with Nahuatl /in).	**ahsi**	to arrive
aik	never	**ahsikamati**	to understand s.t.
akihkeh	those who	**akin**	he who, she who
akin saso	whoever	**altepetl**	town
an	and	**axkan**	now, today
chiya	to wait (nimo); to wait for someone (nik)	**den**	of the (combination of Spanish /de/ and Nahuat/ in)
ihkon	like this	**ikxichiya**	to wait by foot
ilnamiki	to remember s.t.	**in**	the, he who, she who, those who; here
inin	this	**ipan**	on
itskia	to grab, take s.t.	**ittitia**	to show s.o. s.t.

198

ixpan	in front of	**kema**	yes
kokoa	to hurt s.o.	**mak**	on s.o.'s hand
man	imperativo	**mapalewia**	to give a helping hand to s.o.
matilistli	knowledge	**matilkawa**	to forget s.t.
mawisolos	reverence	**mawistika**	in an honored way, honored
mawisyotia	to honor s.t. or s.o.	**melawak**	truly
miak	a lot	**mikawia**	? (unknown translation)
mopowa	to be counted	**moxeloa**	to be divided
namehwan	you all (independent pronoun)	**nan**	here (nikan)
nawak	next to	**neixkwepaloni**	revolution (faces are turned)
neka	over there	**nekahkayawalistli**	deception, trickery
nekate	over there	**nepechteka**	a bow of repect
nesetil netewialoni	unity in battle	**netewilistli**	the fight
nexikoalistli	greed	**ni**	nor
non	that, that which	**nonkes**	those who
noso	or	**ok achi**	more

okichtin	male	**okichtli**	male
pahpakilistli	happiness	**papanoltilia**	to pass s.t. to s.o.
pewaloni	beginnings (used here to mean, principles)	**san**	just
sepan	together	**setilia**	to unite
tech	regarding, up against	**tehwani**	us
teka mokayawa	to make mockery of someone	**tekiti**	to work
tekitki	a worker	**tekohtli**	owner, boss
tekokokayotl	cruelty, torment, enemy	**tewia**	to fight s.o.
tlahtlakolli	sin, fault	**tlahtlaksa**	to force s.o. to work hard or run hard
tlahtoani	governor, ruler	**tlakachiwa**	to respect, make friends with
tlakapowa	to take s.o. into account	**tlalilia**	to place s.t. onto s.o.
tlalle	land	**tlaltikpak**	earth
tlampa	under	**tlanawatille**	a mandate, order
tlanekilistikayopa	with one's will	**tlania**	to ask s.t.
tlasohtla	to love s.o.	**tlasohtlalistli**	love
tlatlani	to win	**tlatlawtia**	to plead with s.o.

tlen	what	**tlipoloa**	to burn and erase
tonochtin	all of us (ti+nochi+tin)	**waxkaitl/ axkaitl**	s.o.'s property
wel	good, well	**weyichiwa**	to become big
yawi	to go	**yehwa**	he, she, it
yewahka	ancient	**yehwan**	they, them
yo	already (ye + o)	**yolewa**	to invite s.o.
yollotl	heart		

24.

Conclusion

Will Nahuatl survive into the future? Although there are many speakers today, Nahuatl is still vulnerable for several reasons. First, there are many regions where Nahuatl is spoken and few of them know of each other's existence. The advancement in technology so far is mostly benefiting people who live in cities, not in rural Nahuatl towns, which still lacks internet service. Within the Huasteca, schooling for the youth has increased, and though there are bilingual programs funded by the government, in practice, few teachers can actually speak Nahuatl and most simply try to teach Spanish instead. Second, many parents are no longer speaking to their kids in Nahuatl. Much like second generation Mexican-Americans who are losing Spanish outside of contact with elders. In Mexico, it is difficult for Nahuas to maintain the home language when work in the cities is in Spanish, and education is mostly in Spanish. Nahuatl is rarely ever used as the language to learn material. While there is much support for ancient indigenous culture within Mexico (a feature which not too long ago was cause for self-shame), there is still little support for marginalized communities and little interest by the mainstream to learn from them. Instead, self-taught elders from the city with no knowledge of spoken Nahuatl have become the new respected elders.

Most native speakers feel it is okay to shame their language because it is already so 'mixed' with Spanish and 'unpure.' You can see why they would say this, there are many words from Spanish that are now in Nahuatl like: para, pero, patox, kawayoh, mopreokuparoa and more. In reality though, there is no such thing as a 'pure' language. In fact, most of the words in English are estimated to be non-English words, and is English endangered today? Not at all. Spanish has hundreds of loan-words from Arabic and English. Japanese has borrowed extensively from English, French and Chinese. Linguistic borrowing is a very normal process and shows you that a language is still healthy and dynamic.

From within the Nahua world, there is also internal debate about which variety should be taught, and which spelling convention should be used. One one extreme, some support writing in a purely phonetic system unlike any that exists in this world, where the writing has to ignore morpheme roots and instead represent the spoken speech as exactly as possible. On another side are those who prefer a historical/traditional perspective in which the writing system represents unity across varieties by showing the roots of every word. In reality, the spelling convention itself matters much less than the divide caused by its debate. Natives could be writing in Latin script, or an idealized Classical Nahuatl script, a spelling system created from new glyphs, or a spin-off of another writing system. The form does not matter as much as unity does. So how does one attain unity?

The ideal method is by consensus. In this view, representatives of different regions would gather and come to an agreement. This is what the Academia de la Lengua Mixteca Ve'e Tu'un Savi has accomplished. This organization is made up of various Mixtec speakers and elders who gather every year. On the other hand, this organization also has no power to enforce their writing system and non-Mixtec people frequently ignore their recommended alphabet. Furthermore, there are several Mixtec activists who dislike the idea of unifying their language through an institution. It is impossible to really gain full consensus.

The most common method of unity for the powerful languages of today (English, Japanese, Spanish) has been through oppression. English is also an old language that was made up of many variations even before it left England. People slowly begin to speak the dialect that is in 'power.' This is what becomes the 'standard language.' The other dialects are sadly deemed inferior or lower-class. Several times power switched regions in England. When this occurred, the new region became the 'standard dialect'. A different model of unity is the one the Basque language is following. Basque also has diverse dialects of their language. In their struggle of revitalization, they have created an artificial language that blends features from each of the different dialects. This method respects diversity while also aiming for unity.

On the bright side, there is much more attention given to Nahuatl revitalization than there has been in the past with increased unify in recent years with the help of social media, YouTube videos and increased activity on Facebook. Large amounts of people from the Huasteca are gathering in online groups, though the language of unity increasingly has become Spanish. The aim is really to make sure the youth value their language and also that parents value their language. There is a lot of support people from abroad could give to Nahuatl. I hope this book can contribute to that.

Answers:

Exercise 2. Answers

1. tlal-li
2. nemilis-tli
3. siwapil
4. kwapuertah
5. tepos-tli
6. tlaltipak-tli
7. ama-tl
8. tlatsotson-tli

Exercise 3. Answers

1. miston - cat
2. mistonmeh - cats
3. okwilimeh - worms
4. pantalon - pants
5. tototl - bird
6. tepetl - hill
7. amatl - paper/papers

Exercise 4. Answers

1. women - siwameh
2. boys - okichpilmeh
3. men - tlakameh
4. fish(es) - michimeh
5. dogs - chichimeh
6. pigs - pitsomeh
7. indigenous people - masewalmeh
8. horses - kawayohmeh
9. cities - altepemeh
10. books - amoxtli/amoxmeh
11. snakes - koameh

Exercise 5. Answers

1. I am a teenage boy - Nitelpokatl
2. You are a teenage boy - Titelpokatl
3. He is a teenage boy - Telpokatl
4. We are teenage boys - Titelpokameh
5. You all are teenage boys - Intelpokameh
6. They are teenage boys - Telpokameh
7. I am a teenage girl - Niichpokatl
8. We are teenage girls - Tiichpokameh
9. They are teenage girls - Ichpokameh
10. He is a young boy - Okichpil
11. They are young boys - Okichpilmeh
12. You are a young girl - Tisiwapil
13. You all are young girls - Insiwapilmeh
14. They are young girls - Siwapilmeh
15. I am a student - Nimomachtihketl
16. You are a student - Timomachtihketl
17. She is a student - Momachtihketl
18. They are students - Momachtianih
19. We are students - Timomachtianih
20. You all are students - Inmomachtianih

Exercise 6. Answers

1. nochichi - my dog (or) It's my dog.
2. nochichiwan - my dogs (or) They're my dogs.
3. motlayi - your uncle (or) He's your uncle.
4. motlayiwan - your uncles (or) They are your uncles.
5. noikniwan - my brothers (or) They are my brothers.
6. iikniwan - his/ her siblings (or) They are his/her siblings.
7. toikniw - our sibling (or) He/She is our sibling.
8. inmoikniw - ya'lls sibling (or) He/She is ya'lls sibling.
9. ininikniw - their sibling (or) He/She is their sibling.
10. ininikniwan - their siblings (or) They are their siblings.
11. mokawayoh - your horse (or) It's your horse.
12. ininpitso - their pig (or) It' their pig.
13. motamal - your tamal (or) It's your tamal.
14. nokoton - my shirt (or) It's my shirt.
15. noew - my bean (or) It's my bean.
16. noaw - my water (or) It's my water.

Exercise 7. Answers

1. my tamal - notamal
2. It's my tamal. - Notamal.
3. your uncle - motlayi
4. their uncle - inintlayi
5. my shirt - nokoton
6. my horses - nokawayohwan
7. our horses - tokawayohwan
8. your shirt - mokoton
9. our dad - totatah
10. your (plural) mom - inmonanan
11. your aunt - moawi
12. She's your aunt. - Moawi.
13. They are your aunts. - Moawiwan.

Exercise 8. Answers

1. I am sick. - Nimokokoa.

2. You are sick. - Timokokoa.
3. He is sick. - Mokokoa.
4. We are sick. - Timokokoah.
5. You all are sick. - Inmokokoah.
6. They are sick. - Mokokoah.
7. I'm eating. - Nitlakwa.
8. You are eating. - Titlakwa.
9. She is eating. - Tlakwa.
10. We are eating. - Titlakwah.
11. You all are eating. - Intlakwah.
12. They are eating. - Tlakwah.
13. I am running. - Nimotlaloa.
14. I am studying. - Nimomachtia.
15. They are studying. - Momachtiah.

Exercise 9. Answers

1. Na nitlakwa. - I eat.
2. Ya momachtia. - He/She is studying.
3. Tohhwantin timotlaloah. - We run.
4. Intlakwah. - You all eat.
5. Nehnemi. - He/She walks.
6. Nehnemih. - They walk.
7. Mohmostla nikochi. - Every day I sleep.
8. Titlahkwiloa. - You write.
9. Kemmantsin titlahkwiloah. - We sometimes write.
10. Inmomachtiah. - You all study.
11.Tohwantin timomachtiah. - We study

Exercise 10. Answers

1. I am eating. - Nitlakwa. (or) Na nitlakwa.
2. You are eating. - Titlakwa. (or) Ta titlakwa.
3. We are eating. - Titlakwah. (or) Tohwantin titlakwah.
4. I am walking. - Ninehnemi. (or) Na ninehnemi.
5. We are walking. - Tinehnemih. (or) Tohwantin tinehnemih.
6. She is running. - Motlaloa. (or) Ya motlaloa.
7. He is writing. - Tlahkwiloa. (or) Ya tlahkwiloa.
8. You all are eating. - Intlakwah. (or) Inmohwantin intlakwah.
9. We are running. - Timotlaloah. (or) Tohwantin timotlaloah.
10. They are studying. - Momachtiah. (or) Inihwantin momachtiah.
11. He is studying. - Momachtia. (or) Ya momachtia.
12. I am studying - Nimomachtia. (or) Na nimomachtia.
13. You sleep everyday. - Mohmostla tikochi. (or) Mohmostla ta tikochi.
14. We sleep every day. - Mohmostla tikochih. (or) Mohmostla tohwantin tikochih.
15. I sometimes study. - Kemmantsin nimomachtia. (or) Kemmantsin na nimomachtia.

Exercise 11. Answers

1. Ma niyaw. - I should go.
2. Xiyaw. - Go!
3. Ma yowi. - He/She should go.
4. Ma tiyakan. - Let's go!
5. Xiwallaw. - Come!
6. Xiwallakan. - You all come!
7. Xichoka. - Cry!
8. Xichokakan. - You all cry!
9. Ma tlaawetsi. - May it rain!
10. Xisanilo. - Speak!
11. Ma ihsa. - He/She should wake up.
12. Ma titlakwakan. - Let's eat!

Exercise 12. Answers

1. Let's dance! - Ma timihtotikan!
2. You dance! - Ximihtoti!
3. Sing! - Xiwika!
4. You all sing! - Xiwikakan.
5. Let's sing! - Ma tiwikakan!
6. Wake up! - Xiihsa!
7. They should sing! - Ma wikakan!
8. He says she should sleep! - Kihtoa ma kochi!
9. Eat! - Xitlakwa.
10. You all eat! - Xitlakwakan!
11. May it be sunny! - Ma tona!

Exercise 13. Answers

1. Itstok Maria. - Maria is present.
2. Axkanah itstok Maria. - Maria isn't present.
3. Eltok se amatl. - There is a paper.
4. Itstok nochichi - My dog is present.
5. Eltok nochan. - My house is present.
6. Itstok se tlakatl. - There is a man (present)
7. Axonkah atl. - There's no water.
8. Onkah tlakwalli? - Is there food?

Exercise 14. Answers

1. Is she here? - Itstok?
2. Is it here? - Eltok?
3. Here is a chair. - Nikan eltok kwasiyah.
4. Here are two chairs. - Nikan eltok ome kwasiyah.
5. The chair is not here. - Axkanah eltok kwasiyah (or) Axeltok kwasiyah (or) amo eltok kwasiyah.
6. There are no chairs. - Axkanah onkah kwasiyah (or) Axonkah kwasiyah (or) Amo onkah kwasiyah.
7. There's no problem. - Axkanah onkah kwalantli (or) Axonkah kwalantli (or) Amo onkah kwalantli.
8. Is there a question? - Onkah se tlahtlanilistli?
9. There's work. - Onkah tekitl.
10. Here is a bed. - Nikan eltok tlapechtli.

Exercise 15. Answers

1. Nikochis tlayowa. - I'll sleep at night.
2. Amo kochiseh. - They won't sleep.
3. Axkanah timihtotiseh. - We won't dance.
4. Mostla amo tlaawetsis. - It won't rain tomorrow.
5. Ayikana nitlakwas. - I won't eat yet.
6. Ayokkana nimihtotis. - I won't dance any more.
7. Axakah wikas. - No one will sing.
8. Tiwikaseh senyowal. - We will sing all night.
9. Amo tiwikas mostla. - You won't sing tomorrow.
10. Ayoktichokaseh. - We won't cry any more.

Exercise 16. Answers

1. Tomorrow I'll sleep. - Mostla nikochis.
2. Tomorrow we will run. - Mostla timotlaloseh.
3. It's going to rain all night. - Tlaawetsis senyowal.
4. You will sleep at night. - Tikochis tlayowa.
5. You won't sleep at night. - Amo tikochis tlayowa.
6. We will dance all night. - Timihtotiseh senyowal.
7. We will speak tomorrow. - Tisaniloseh mostla.
8. They will wake up tomorrow. - Ihsaseh mostla.
9. I will run tomorrow. - Nimotlalos mostla.
10. I won't eat tomorrow. - Amo nitlakwas mostla.
11. The moon will shine all night. - Metstonas senyowal.
12. The moon won't shine at night. - Amo metstonas tlayowa.

Exercise 17. Answers

1. Who are you? - Akkiya ta?
2. Who is she? - Akkiya ya?
3. Who is he? - Akkiya ya?
4. Who are they? - Akkiya ininhwantin?
5. Where are you from? - Kanin tiwallaw?
6. Where do you originate? - Kanin tiewa?
7. How many dogs do you have? - Keski chichimeh tikinpiya?
8. When is Juan coming? - Kemman wallas Juan?
9. What do you eat? - Tlen tikkwa?
10. Why do you dance? - Kenke timihtotia?
11. Why do you learn Nahuatl? - Kenke timomachtia Nahuatl?
12. Why don't you like comedians? - Kenke amo tikinamati kamanaloanih?

Exercise 18. Answers

1. Jalisco - On the surface of the sand.
2. Zapotlan - Place of zapote fruit
3. Michoacan. - Place of owners of fish.
4. Oaxaca. - On the nose of guaje pod trees.
5. Chiapas. - Place of chia seeds.
6. Guatemala. - Place of wood piles (or) Place that's wood filled.
7. Chicontepec. - Place of seven hills.
8. Cuernavaca. - Next to the forest.
9. Tula. - Place of rush/tules.
10. Chapultepec. - On grasshopper hill.
11. Ajuchitlan. - Place of watery flower.

Exercise 19. Answers

1. saniloa. intransitive.
2. sanilwia. transitive.
3. kwa. transitive
4. wallaw. intransitive.
5. tlakwa. intransitive.
6. tlatla. intransitive.
7. tlatia. transitive.
8. tlehko. intransitive.
9. toka. transitive.
10. toka. intransitive. (because there are two versions of this verb)

Exercise 20. Answers

1. Nikihtoa. - I say (it).
2. Tikihtoa. - You say.
3. Tikihtoah. - We say.
4. Inkihtoah. - You all say.
5. Nikihtos. - I will say.
6. Tikihtoseh. - We will say.
7. Inkisewia. - You all turn it off.
8. Tiksewiah. - We turn it off.
9. Kisewiseh. - They will turn it off.
10. Nikneki. - I want it.
11. Niknekis. - I will want it.
12. Nikchiwas. - I will do it.
13. Nikamati nimihtotis. - I like to dance.
14. Nikamati niwikas. - I like to sing.
15. Tikamatih tiwikaseh. - We like to sing.

Exercise 21. Answers

1. I like him/her. - Nikamati.
2. You like him/her. - Tikamati.
3. He likes her. - Kiamati / kamati.
4. She likes him. - Kiamati / kamati.
5. We like her. - Tikamatih.
6. They like him. - Kiamatih / kamatih.
7. I want it. - Nikneki.
8. You love him. - Tikneki.
9. You do it. - Tikchiwa.
10. They do it. - Kichiwah.
11. You all do it. - Inkichiwah.
12. I do it. - Nikchiwa.
13. I turn it off. - Niksewia.

Exercise 22. Answers

1. Tinotatah. - You are my father.
2. Tinonanan. - You are my mother.
3. Nonanan. - She is my mother. (or) my mother
4. Notatah. - He is my father. (or) my father
5. Noichpokaw. - She is my teenage daughter. (or) my daughter
6. Toichpokaw. - She is our teenage daughter. (or) our daughter
7. Toichpokawan. - They are our teenage daughters (or) our daughters
8. Notatahhwan. - They are our parents. (or) our parents
9. Itelpokaw. - He is his son. (or) his/her teenage son
10. Itelpokawan. - They are his sons. (or) his/her teenage sons
11. Ininmachikniwan. - They are their cousins. (or) their cousins
12. Tokonewan. - They are our children. (or) our children
13. Inmokonewan. - They are ya'lls children. (or) ya'lls children
14. Nototatah. - He/she is my grandfather (or my grandfather
15. Nototatahwan. - They are my grandparents (or) my grandparents
16. Tiikonew Maria? - Are you Maria's daughter?

Exercise 23. Answers

1. You are my sister. - Tinoweltih.
2. Is she your sister? - Moweltih?
3. He is your young man. - Motelpokaw.
4. They are your young girls. - Moichpokawan.
5. He is your little boy. - Mookichpil.
6. She is your little girl. - Mosiwapil.
7. It's our land. - Totlalwi.
8. Is she your student? - Momomachtikah?
9. Is she your teacher? - Motlamachtikah?
10. They are my teachers. - Notlamachtikawan.
11. He is my grandfather. - Nototatah.
12. They are my grandparents. - Nototatahwan.
13. Ya'll are my children. - Innokonewan.
14. Are you Maria's child? - Tiikonew Maria?
15. Are you Juan's father? - Tiitatah Juan?
16. Lukas, I am your father. - Lukas, nimotatah.

Exercise 24. Answers

1. You are my student. - Tinomomachtihkaw.
2. You are my teacher. - Tinotlamachtihkaw.
3. I am your student. - Nimomomachtihkaw.
4. I am your teacher. - Nimotlamachtihkaw.
5. You all are my teachers. - Innotlamachtihkawan.

Exercise 25. Answers

1. A giver to people. - Temakaketl.
2. A giver of things.   - Tlamakaketl.
3. A seller of things.   - Tlanamakaketl.
4. A receiver of stuff. - Tlaselihketl.
5. A dancer. - Mihtotihketl.
6. A believer (of stuff). - Tlaneltokaketl.
7. A visitor (of people). - Tepaxalohketl.
8. A drunkard. - Iwintiketl.
9. A shouter. - Tsahtsiketl.

Exercise 26. Answers

1. Xinechilli. - Tell me.
2. Xinechchiya. - Wait for me.
3. Nimitschiyas. - I will wait for you.
4. Nimitsillia. - I tell you.
5. Kena nimitskwamachilia. - I do understand you.
6. Naman nikkwamachilia. - Now I understand it.
7. Amo nimechkwamachilia. - I don't understand you all.
8. Nimitsneki. - I love/need you.
9. Tinechneki? - Do you love/need me?
10. Xikilli. - Tell him/her.
11. Nimechillis. - I will tell you all.
12. Xinechchiyakan. - You all wait for me!
13. Tikkwamachilia? - Do you understand it/him/her?
14. Timitskokoliah. - We hate you.
15. Innechkokoliah? - Do you all hate me?

Exercise 27. Answers

1. I hate it. - Nikkokolia.
2. I hate you. - Nimitskokolia.
3. I hate them. - Nikinkokolia.
4. You hate me. - Tinechkokolia.
5. You hate him. - Tikkokolia.
6. You hate them. - Tikinkokolia.
7. Do you hate us? - Titechkokolia?
8. Will you wait for me? - Tinechchiyas?
9. Will you wait for us? - Titechchiyas?
10. Now I understand (it) - Naman nikkwamachilia.
11. Do they want us? - Technekih?
12. They will tell me. - Nechilliseh.
13. She will tell you today. - Naman mitsillis.
14. He won't wait for you. - Amo mitschiyas.
15. We will wait for you. - Timitschiyaseh.
16. Does he understand it? - Kikwamachilia?

Exercise 28. Answers

1. It is understood. Mokwamachilia.
2. It is said. Moillia (or) Moilwia.
3. Maria and I see each other. - Maria wan na timoittah.
4. I cut myself. - Nimoteki.
5. I sit down. - Nimosewia.
6. I tell myself. - Nimoillia.
7. We talk to each other. - Timosanilwiah.

Exercise 29. Answers

1. spiky - witstik
2. flowery - xochitik
3. bloody - estik
4. young looking woman - ixichpokatik
5. indigenous looking face - ixmasewaltik
6. non-indigenous looking face - ixkoyotik
7. dark/black in complexion - ixyayawitik
8. round-faced - ixyawaltik

Exercise 30. Answers

1. Nikittak. - I saw it.
2. Tikittakeh. - We saw it.
3. Kiittakeh. - They saw it.
4. Intlakwahkeh? - Did you all eat?
5. Ixpoliwkeh. - They disappeared.
6. Mikeh. - They died.
7. Mikki. - He/she died.
8. Inmotenxinkeh. - You all shaved.
9. Motenxinki. - He/she shaved.
10. Ya nimaltih. - I've already showered.
11. Maltihkeh. - They showered.
12. Maltihki. - He/she showered.
13. Maltih. - He/she showered.
14. Intlakwahkeh. - You all ate.
15. Ya titlakwahkeh. - We already ate.
16. Mokokohkeh. - They were sick.

Exercise 31. Answers

1. You fell. - Tiwetski.
2. We fell. - Tiwetskeh.
3. He fell. - Wetski.
4. They fell. - Wetskeh.
5. You woke up. - Tiihsak.
6. She woke up. - Ihsak.
7. They woke up. - Ihsakeh.
8. I got out. - Nikiski.
9. Ya'll got out. - Inkiskeh.
10. It disappeared. - Ixpoliwki.
11. They disappeared. - Ixpoliwkeh.
12. You disappeared. - Tiixpoliwki.
13. He died. - Mikki.
14. They died. - Mikkeh.
15. I walked. - Ninehnenki.
16. She ate. - Tlakwahki.
17. They ate. - Tlakwahkeh.

Exercise 32. Answers

1. full of corn - sinyoh
2. full of itch - ahwayoh
3. full of lice - atinyoh (the last /i/ is weak, leaving the m by itself)
4. full of grass - sakayoh
5. its weight - ietikayo
6. a lie - istlakatiyotl
7. a photograph - ixkopinkayotl

Exercise 33. Answers

1. I saw an owl. - Nikittak se tekolotl.
2. Did you see that spider? - Tikittak ne/inon/nopa tokatl?
3. I'm observing the eagle. - Niktlachilia kwawtli.
4. Grab that mouse! - Xikitski ne/inon/nopa kimichin!
5. The snake is eating a mouse. - Koatl kikwa kimichin.

Exercise 34. Answers

1. I plant sweet potato. - Nikamohsaka.
2. I transport water. - Niasaka.
3. I sell corn. - Nisinsaka.
4. I cut trees. - Nikwateki.
5. I drink medicine. - Nipahoni.
6. I sell medicine. - Nipahnamaka.
7. Internet. - Tepostokatsawalli.
8. male dog. - Okichchichi.
9. male cat. -Okichmiston.
10. female cat. - Siwamiston.
11. zapote fruit tree. - Tsapokwawitl.
12. orange fruit tree. - Alaxoxkwawitl.
13. banana tree. - Kwaxilokwawitl.
14. I'm lazy (dying from lazyness). - Nitlatsmiki.

Exercise 35. Answers

1. tsahtsik - J
2. tsahtsiseh - I
3. nikmakakka - A
4. tikmakakehya - B
5. kikwik - E
6. kikwikeh - F
7. niwetskak - H
8. wetskak - G
9. mopatlak - D
10. nikpatlak - C

Exercise 36. Answers

1. mokawki - H
2. mokawkeh - G
3. tikalakki - B
4. tikalakkeh - A
5. nitlachichinki - F
6. tlachichinkeh - E
7. kena weli - C
8. axniweli - D
9. kipixki - J
10. tikpixkeh - I

Exercise 37. Answers

1. Nechpaxaloskia pero axmoahxilia. - He would visit me but he doesn't have time.
2. Nimitstlaxtlawiliskia pero axonkah tomin. - I would pay you but there's no money.
3. Nikkowaskia tlan nikpiyaskia tomin. - I would buy it if I had money.
4. Tiktlachiliskiah tlamawisolli pero ya axkineki. - We would watch a movie but he/he doesn't want to.
5. Tiktlachiliyayah tlamawisolli. - We were watching a movie.
6. Nikoniyaya chichik. - I was drinking beer.
7. Kanin eltok noyaves? - Where are your keys?
8. Eltos yankwik tlamawisolli. - There will be a new movie.
9. Eltoya se amoxtli, pero axnikahsi. - There was a book but I can't find it.
10. Ayokkana tiihkatoseh. - We won't be standing anymore.

Exercise 38. Answers

1. I would do it if I could - Nikchiwaskia tlan niweliskia.
2. I would eat if I were hungry. - Nitlakwaskia tlan nimayanaskia.
3. We would stay if we weren't busy. - Timokawaskiah tlan amo timotekiwiskiah.
4. I was eating when you called me. - Nitlakwayaya kemman tinechnohnotski.
5. We used to watch t.v. - Tiktlachiliyayah tlamawisolli.
6. I would sleep now but I can't. - Nikochiskia sanpampa axniweli.
7. They used to sleep early, not anymore. - Kochiyayah kwalkan, ayokkana.
8. He is asleep. - Kochtok.
9. He will be asleep if you call him. - Kochtos tlan tiknohnotsas.
10. She had been asleep when you called her. - Kochtoya kemman tiknohnotski.

Exercise 39. Answers

1. Xikselih ni koskatl. B
2. Nimitstlahpalos. F
3. Xinechpalewi. E
4. Ximaltiya. C
5. Nechpaktia nimaltis. H
6. Nechpaktia nimihtotis. G
7. Ayikana xikmikti. A
8. Amo nechneltokilia. I
9. Tlen tikmachilia? J
10. Akkiya nechpalewis? D

Exercise 40. Answers

1. Nikontekis mankoh. - I'm going to cut mango.
2. Mohmostla nikwalteki mankoh. - Everyday I come cut mangos.
3. Xikontisi sintli. - Go grind corn!
4. Ma tikontisikan sintli. - Let's go grind corn!
5. Momachtiti. - He's going to go (there) to study.
6. Momachtito. - He went over there to study.
7. Momachtiki. - He went over there to study.
8. Momachtiko. - He came here to study.
9. Momachtikoh. - They came here to study.
10. Amo ximomachtiti. - Don't go to study.

Exercise 41. Answers

1. She went (over there) to sell stuff. - Tlanamakato.
2. I came (here) to sell stuff. - Nitlanamakako.
3. We came (here) to buy stuff. - Titlakowakoh.
4. Tomorrow I will come here to buy stuff. - Mostla nitlakowaki.
5. Tomorrow they will come here to sleep. - Mostla kochikih.
6. I'm going over there to sleep. - Nikochiti.
7. I'm going to sleep (over there) - Nionkochis.
8. Go (over there) to call your dad. - Xiknotsati motatah (or) Xikonnotsati motatah.

Exercise 42. Answers

1. Nechnotstiwallaw. She comes calling me.
2. Nechnotstiw. She goes calling me.
3. Kikwahtiwetski. He ate it (suddenly).
4. Tlakwahtikah. He is eating.
5. Tlakwahtihkak. He continues eating (He's standing eating).
6. Tlaonitinemi. She's drinking (here and there).
7. Nikkowatewas. I'm going to buy it (before leaving).
8. Kikwahtikiski. He ate it (on the way somewhere).

Exercise 43. Answers

1. She's singing here and there. Wikatinemi.
2. They are singing here and there. Wikatinemih.
3. They were walking here and there. Nehnentinemiyayah.
4. He's studying right now. Momachtihtikah.
5. They're studying right now. Momachtihtikateh.
6. She comes whistling. Kikistiwallaw.
7. She goes whistling. Kikistiw.
8. She suddenly screamed. Tsahtsitiwetski.

Exercise 44. Answers

1. I'll start reading. Pewas nitlapowas. (or) Nipewas nitlapowas.
2. I finished reading. Tlanki nitlapowa. (or) Nitlanki nitlapowa.
3. I'll start writing. Pewas nitlahkwilos (or) Nipewas nitlahkwilos.
4. I finished writing. Tlanki nitlahkwilos. (or) Nitlanki nitlahkwilos.
5. She can write. Weli tlahkwilos.

Exercise 45. Answers

1. I will buy a tortilla. Nikkowas tlaxkalli.
2. I will buy you a tortilla. Nimitskowis tlaxkalli.
3. I sell clothes. Niknamaka yoyomitl.
4. I will sell clothes to you. Nimitsnamakiltis yoyomitl.
5. I cry. Nichoka.
6. You make me cry. Tinechchokiltia.
7. Money is lacking. Poliwi tomin.
8. I'm lacking money. Nechpoloa tomin.
9. She comes out. Kisa.
10. He takes her out. Kikixtia.
11. You die. Timiki.
12. I kill you. Nimitsmiktia.

Exercise 46. Answers

1. I will eat you. Nimitskwas.
2. I will eat your tortillas. Nimitskwalilis motlaxkal.
3. I will make you eat tortillas. Nimitskwaltis tlaxkalli.
4. I work. Nitekiti.
5. I employ it (I use it). Niktekiwia.
6. You take out the metate. Tikkixtia metlatl.
7. You take the metate from me. Tinechkixtilia metlatl.
8. She tastes the food. Kimachilia tlakwalli.
9. She gives me food to taste. Nechmachiltia tlakwalli.

Exercise 47. Answers

1. Sewetsi. Tlasewetsi.
2. Totonik. Tlatotoniya.
3. Pitsawkawetsi. Tlapitsawkawetsi.
4. Achichipika. Tlaachichipika. (it's raining lightly, dripping)
5. Eheka (it's windy). Tlaeheka.
6. Ayowi. Tlaayowa (it's foggy).

Exercise 48. Answers

1. He will get big. Weyiyas.
2. I will get fat. Nitomawas.
3. It got lower. Echkapaniwki.
4. I will not get any taller. Ayokniwahkapantiyas.
5. She will sturdy herself to pick something up. Motetiyas.

Answers

Vocabulary List

achi	a little	**akasotik**	light in weight; quick to act
achikwalli	it's better that...	**akatl**	reed
achitsin	a tiny bit	**akkiya**	who
achiyo	a piece of s.t.	**akkiyaweli**	whoever
achiyok	a little more	**akoatl**	water snake
achtowi	first	**alaxiwi**	To slide (Ni) (Class 2)
achtowiya	that one time	**alaxox**	orange fruit
ahachi	in small amounts	**altepetl**	city
ahachika	often	**altia**	To bathe s.o. (Nik) (Class 3)
ahawilli	toy	**amati**	To like s.t. or s.o. (Nik) (Class 2)
ahki	To swim (Ni) (Class 1)	**amatl**	paper
ahkokwi	To put away s.t. (Nik) (Class 1)	**amaxalli**	river fork
ahkolli	shoulder	**amelli**	spring, well
ahkomana	To become frightened (Typically said of a group) (Class 2)	**ameya**	For water to flow (Class 2)
ahkwexoa	To sneeze (Ni) (Class 3)	**amiki**	To be thirsty (Ni) (Class 2)
ahsi	To be able to reach (Ni); To reach or find something (Nik) (Class 1)	**amo**	no
		amoxtli	book
ahwa	To scold someone (Nik) (Class 1)	**analli**	lake shore; land on other side of water
ahwa	To bark (Tla) (Class 1)	**anke**	he who, she who, those who
ahwayoh	itchy	**apachtli**	palm tree
ahwayowa	To have an itch (Ni) (Class 2)	**apismiki**	To be hungry (Ni) (Class 2)
ahwiak	delicious; good smelling	**apole**	Black Cherry
ahxilia	To catch up to (Nik); To have free time (Nimo) (Class 3)	**asaka**	To transport water (Ni) (Class 1)
		asetl	hail
ahxitia	To complete s.t. (Nik); To complete your birthday (Nik) (Class 3)	**asultik**	blue
akahya	someone		

ateka	To pour water (Ni) (Class 1)	axmero	not much
atik	watery	axtlen	nothing; you're welcome
atimitl	lice; louse	ayatl	net
atiya	To melt (Class 2)	ayawtli	fog
atl	water	ayi	not yet
atlak	could it be?	ayikanah	not yet
atlawtli	river, stream	ayo	something's broth, juice
atli	To drink water (Ni) (Class 1)	ayohtli	squash
atolli	atole corn drink	ayokkanah	no longer
atototl	heron, water bird	ayokmo	no longer
awakatl	avocado	ayotl	turtle
awi	aunt, ma'am	ayotochin	armadillo
awiltia	To play with s.t. (Nik); To sexually assault someone (Nik) (Class 3)	ayowalli	lagoon
		ayowitl	fog
awitl	aunt	borroh	donkey
axalli	sand	chacha	dragon fruit
axika	nowhere	chamani	to sprout (Class 2)
axixtli	urine	chamolin	scarlet parrot
axkaitl	property	chantli	home
axkanah	no	chapolin	grasshopper
axkanelin	ant	chektik	spoiled child
axke	right?	cheneh	too much
axkemman	never	chichi	dog
axkeniwki	doesn't matter	chichi	To suckle (Ni) (Class 1)
axkenke	just because	chichik	alcohol
axmas	not much		

223

chichik	bitter
chichiltik	red
chichina	To suck s.t. (Nik); To smoke tobacco (Nik) (Class 2)
chichinoa	To burn s.t. completely (Nik) (Class 3)
chichipika	To drip (Class 1)
chichitl	breast
chichiwalli	breast
chikawak	hard, strong
chikiwitl	basket
chiko	crooked, out of line, off the road
chikome	7
chikwase	6
chikweyi	8
chikweyiya	last week
chikwnawi	9
chilli	chili
chilmolli	salsa, sauce
chimalin	round device used to shuck corn
chinanko	neighborhood, village
chipawak	white
chiwa	To do s.t. (Nik) (Class 2)
chiya	To wait for s.t. (Nik); To wait (Nimo) (Class 2)
chiyaktik	greasy
chiyawak	greasy
chocho	younger sibling
choka	To cry (Ni) (Class 1)
chokolatl	chocolate
chokoxtik	blond
choloa	To flee (Ni) (Class 3)
chololtia	To make someone flee (nik) (Class 3)

echkapantik	short
ehekatl	air, wind
eheliwis	all over
eheyi	three of each
ekawilli	shade
ekawillotl	shade
eli	To be (Ni); For plants or hair to grow; To transform (Ni) (Class 2)
elmoyawi	To be nauseous (Ni) (Class 2)
elpotsa	To burp s.o. (Nik); To burp yourself (Nimo) (Class 2)
eltlapal	wing
elwikatl	sky
enel	bean filled corn cakes
epatl	skunk
espoloa	To apply blood to s.t. (Typically in ceremonies) (Nik) (Class 3)
esso	blood (of someone)
estli	blood
etik	heavy
etika	something's weight
etiya	To become heavy (Ni) (Class 2)
etsatl	wasp
ewa	To originate from (Ni) (Class 2)
ewa	To get up (Nimo); To get s.o. up (Nik) (Class 2)
eyi	3
fierohtik	ugly
ichkayolli	period, mole

ichpokatik looking like a teenage girl

ichpokatl teenage girl

ichtakatsin quietly

ichteki To steal s.t. (Nik) (Class 2)

ihiya To be nauseous from s.t. (Nik) (Class 2)

ihka To be standing (Niihkatok)

ihkopi To shut your eyes, blink (Ni) (Class 2)

ihkwiloa To write s.t. (Nik); To write in general (Nitla) (Class 3)

ihnekwi To smell s.t. (Nik) (Class 2)

ihsa To wake up (Ni) (Class 1)

ihsiwi To hurry (Ni) (Class 2)

ihsiwiltia To hurry someone (Nik) (Class 3)

ihsotla To vomit on s.o. (Nik) (Class 1)

ihti stomach

ihtik inside of

ihtikokoa For something to hurt your stomach (nech) (Class 3)

ihtoa To say s.t. (Nik) (Class 3)

ihtoma To untie s.t. (Nik) (Class 2)

ihtosneki to mean s.t. (Ki) (Class 2)

ihtsoma To sew, embroider s.t. (Nik) (Class 2)

ihwiya had gone

ihwiyo body hair

ihwiyoh hairy

ihxitia To wake s.o. (Nik) (Class 3)

ihyexa To fart on s.o. (Class 2)

ihyokisa To fart (Ni) (Class 2)

ihyotilana To inhale (Ni) (Class 2)

ihyowia To put up with, withstand (Nik) (Class 3)

ikati To fit (Ni) (Class 2)

iknelia To have affection or care for s.o. (Nik) (Class 3)

ikni sibling

iknotsin orphan

ikpowia To carry s.t. on your head (Nik) (Class 3)

ikxi foot, leg

ikxiistitl toenail

ikxisepowi To feel numbness in leg (Ni) (Class 2)

ikxopilli toe

ilkawa To forget s.t. (Nik) (Class 2)

illamiki To remember s.t. (Nik) (Class 2)

illia To tell s.o. s.t. (Nik) (Class 3)

ilpi To be tied up (ilpitok)

ilpia To tie s.t. (Nik) (Class 3)

ilwichiwa To host a party (Ni) (Class 2)

ilwitl party, festival

inama To charge s.o. with money (Nik) (Class 2)

inihwantin they, them

inin this

inmohwantin you all

inon that

iskaltia To raise s.o. (nik) (Class 3)

istaltik pale

istatl	salt
istitl	fingernail
istlakati	To lie (Ni) (Class 2)
istlakawia	To lie to s.o. (Nik) (Class 3)
istlakayotl	a lie
itonalkisa	To sweat (Class 2)
itonalli	sweat
itskia	To grab, touch s.t. (Nik) (Class 3)
itta	To see s.t. (Nik) (Class 1)
iwinti	To be drunk (Ni) (Class 1)
iwintia	To get s.o. drunk (nik) (Class 3)
iwkatsan	even though
iwki	like this or that
iwkinin	like this
iwkinon	like that
iwksi	To ripen, become cooked (Class 2)
ixayo	tear
ixihwiyo	eyelash
ixillamiki	To remember a face (Nik) (Class 2)
ixka	To cook over the fire (nik) (Class 3)
ixko	on top of
ixmati	To recognize s.o. (Nik) (Class 2)
ixmina	For light to blind s.o. (Nech) (Class 2)
ixneska	something's color, appearance
ixpa	To put makeup on s.o. (Nik)
ixpan	in front of
ixpano	To disrespect s.o. (Nik) (Class 1)
ixseltik	tender; looking young
ixtemi	For something to be filled up (Class 1)
ixtemo	To go down a slope or stairs (Ni)
ixteskatl	glasses
ixtiyolli	eye
ixtlamati	To be smart from study (Ni) (Class 2)
ixtolontik	round faced
ixwa	For plants or hair to grow (Class 1)
ixwi	To feel full from eating (Ni) (Class 1)
ixwiw	grandchild
ixxayaktli	face
ixyawaltik	round faced
iyoka	apart
kafen	coffee
kafentik	brown
kahkayawa	To trick s.o. (Nik) (Class 2)
kahtsotl	jicama
kakaahko	up there
kakaliwi	For s.t. to toast (Class 2)
kakaloa	To toast s.t. (nik) (Class 3)
kakanika	where?
kakaoh	cacao beans
kakatsoa	To toast s.t. (Nik) (Class 3)
kakawatl	peanut
kaki	To hear s.t. (Nik) (Class 2)
kakilistli	sound
kakisti	For s.t. to make a sound (Class 1)

kakiwi	To fit (Ni) (Class 2)
kalaki	To enter (Ni) (Class 2)
kallapoa	To open a door (Ni) (Class 3)
kalli	house
kalolo	armadillo
kaltsakwa	To close a door (ni) (Class 2)
kamachalli	jawbone
kamak	mouth
kamanalli	jokes
kamanaloa	To joke around (Ni) (Class 3)
kamapahpaka	To brush your teeth (Ni) (Class 1)
kamapotewi	For one's breath to smell (Ni) (Class 2)
kamati	To talk (Ni) (Class 1)
kamatl	mouth, mouthful
kamatlatla	For your mouth to burn from spicy food (Ni) (Class 1)
kamawia	To speak with s.o. (Nik) (Class 3)
kamohtik	purple
kamohtli	yam
kampa	where
kampaweli	anywhere
kampeka	ceremony
kan	where
kanah	perhaps
kanahya	somewhere
kaneka	way out there
kanin	where
kanke	where
kapana	To slap s.t. (nik) (Class 2)
kapani	For something make a slapping sound (Class 2)

katlani	down there
katlinya	which
kawa	To leave s.t. or s.o. (Nik); To stay (Nimo) (Class 2)
kawayoh	horse
kawilia	To leave s.t. for s.o. (Nik) (Class 3)
kaxania	To loosen s.t. (Nik); For medicine to heal one (Nech) (Class 3)
kaxitl	small bowl
kaxtolli	15
kaxtolliya	two weeks ago
kechkwayo	neck
kekeloa	To tickle s.o. (Nik) (Class 3)
kemelawa	possibly
kemman	when
kemmantika	sometimes
kemmantsin	sometimes
kemmanweli	whenever
kemmanya	sometimes
ken	how
ken se	as if ...; like a....
kena	yes
keniwkatik	What color is...
keniwki	how
kenke	why
kenne	like that
kenni	like this
kennopa	like that
kentia	To dress s.o. (nik) (Class 3)
kentsin	a tiny bit
kenwak	like, as

kenweli	however (in anyway)	konepiya	To give birth (Ni) (Class 2)
keski	how many	konetl	child
ketsa	To stand s.t. (Nik); To stand yourself up (Nimo) (Class 2)	konewah	pregnant person
kewkinon	like that	konewahtiya	To become pregnant (Ni) (Class 2)
kikisi	To whistle (Ni) (Class 2)	kopalli	copal
kil	supposedly		
kimichin	mouse	kopewa	To detach s.t. (Nik) (Class 2)
kisa	To exit, come out (Ni) (Class 2)	kopewi	For s.t. to detatch (Class 2)
kitl	supposedly	kopina	To pull s.t. off; copy (nik) (Class 2)
kixtia	To take s.t. out (Nik) (Class 3)	kopini	For s.t. to become unstuck (Class 2)
kixtilia	To take s.t. from s.o. (Nik); To take s.t. off from s.o. (Nik) (Class 3)	koskatl	necklace
koatl	snake	kosolin	crawfish
kochi	To sleep (Ni) (Class 2)		
kochmiki	To be sleepy (Ni) (Class 2)	kostik	yellow
kocho	small parrot	kotomitl	shirt, blouse
kochteka	To put a baby to sleep (Nik) (Class 2)	kotona	To break s.t. like string, rope (nik) (Class 2)
kokitl	firefly	kotoni	For s.t. to break, like string, rope (nik) (Class 2)
kokoa	To hurt s.o. (Nik); For a part of your body to hurt (Nech) (Class 3)		
kokoa	To hurt s.o. (Nik); To be sick (Nimo) (Class 3)	kotontia	To dress s.o. (nik) (Class 3)
kokok	spicy	kototstsin	short
kokolia	To hate s.o. (Nik) (Class 3)	kowa	To buy s.t. (Nik) (Class 2)
kokoliskwi	To catch a sickness (Ni) (Class 1)	kowia	To buy s.t. for s.o. (Nik) (Class 3)
kokolistli	sickness	kowilia	To buy s.t. for or from s.o. (Nik) (Class 3)
kokotl	pimple, sore		
kokoxkati	To feel weak (Ni) (Class 2)	koxtalli	burlap bag
kokoxmaka	To make an animal weak by overpetting it (Nik) (Class 1)	koyonia	To make a hole in s.t. (Nik) (Class 3)
		koyotik	acting like a non-native
komaleh	co-mother (used to greet female friend with respect)	koyotl	non-native man; city-person
komalli	griddle comal	kwa	To eat s.t. (Nik) (Class 4)
komitl	clay jug		
kompaleh	co-father (used to greet male friend with respect)	kwachenche	woodpecker
		kwahkwalo	To have body cramps (Ni) (Class 1)

kwahkwati	To be sore from working (Ni) (Class 2)
kwaitl	head
kwaixpoyawi	To get dizzy (Ni) (Class 2)
kwakwi	For something to fit your head (Nech) (Class 1)
kwalani	To get angry (Ni) (Class 2)
kwalantli	problem
kwalilia	To eat s.o.'s food (Nik) (Class 3)
kwalkantsin	6-9 am
kwalkanya	3-5 am
kwalli	good
kwalo	For something to be eaten up (such as a cavity, moon, fruit) (Class 1)
kwaltiya	To recover, be repaired (Ni) (Class 2)
kwaltlalia	To repair s.t.; prepare food (Nik) (Class 3)
kwamachilia	To understand s.t. (Nik) (Class 3)
kwamahkawa	To throw s.t.; To throw s.t. away (Nik) (Class 2)
kwamomohtli	owl
kwapa	To turn s.t. over (Nik); To return (Nimo) (Class 2)
kwapelech	rooster
kwapilia	To return s.t. to s.o. (Nik) (Class 3)
kwapitsotl	wild boar
kwapoloa	To be confused, lost, make a mistake (Nimo) (Class 3)
kwasemalotl	rainbow
kwaseso	brain
kwasiyah	chair
kwatehteki	To cut s.o.'s hair (Nik) (Class 2)
kwatenno	toilet
kwatetik	having difficulty in understanding
kwatitlan	forest
kwatlehko	To climb a tree (Ni) Class 1)
kwatochin	rabbit
kwatsahtsi	To shout (Ni) (Class 1)
kwawitl	tree; wood; stick
kwawtli	eagle; hawk
kwaxitlani	To slip and fall (Ni) (Class 2)
kwayo	tree's branch
kweitl	skirt
kweponi	To bloom (Class 2)
kwesiwi	To get bored or fed up (Ni) (Class 2)
kwesoa	For s.t. to worry you (Nech); To be sad (Nimo) (Class 3)
kwesolli	sadness
kwetla	rash-causing worm
kwi	To grab s.t. (Nik) (Class 1)
kwilia	To take s.t. from s.o. (Nik) (Class 3)
kwitewa	To get startled (Nimo) (Class 2)
kwitlatl	poop
lechih	milk
maahsi	To be able to reach with your hands (Ni) (Class 1)
machiknitl	cousin
machilia	To feel, try, taste s.t. (nik) (Class 3)
machilka	something's taste
machkonetl	niece, nephew
machtia	To teach (Nik); To learn (Nimo) (Nik) (Class 3)
mahkawa	To throw s.t. (Nik) (Class 2)

mahmawi	To be afraid (Ni) (Class 2)	**mati**	To know (Nik) (Class 2)
mahmawtia	To scare (Nik) (Class 3)	**mawa**	To infect s.o. (Nik) (Class 2)
mahpilli	fingernail	**mawilia**	To fear (Nik) (Class 3)
mahtlaktli	10	**mawiltia**	To play (Ni) (Class 3)
maihtoa	To pray (Nimo) (Class 3)	**mawisoa**	To be amazed by (Nech) (Class 3)
maitl	hand	**maxixa**	To pee (Ni) (Class 2)
maka	I meant to say...	**maxixmiki**	To really need to pee (Ni) (Class 2)
maka	To give to s.o. (Nik) (Class 1)	**mayana**	To be hungry (Ni) (Class 2)
makahsi	To fear s.t. (Nik) (Class 1)	**mehmeltia**	To sob in crying (Ni) (Class 3)
makawa	To give permission (Nik) (Class 2)	**mekatl**	rope
makilia	To hit s.o. (Nik) (Class 3)	**melawa**	probably
makwah	Well then...	**melawa**	To straighten s.t. ; For men to find each other on the road. (Class 2)
makwilli	5	**melawak**	trully, truth
maltia	To shower, bathe (Ni) (Class 3)	**melpotsa**	To burp (Ni) (Class 2)
malwia	To take special care of (Nik) (Class 3)	**metlatl**	metate grinding stone
malwilli	sacred, delicate, guarded secret	**metstli**	moon, month
mama	To carry s.t. on your back (Nik) (Class 4)	**metstona**	For the moon to shine (Class 1)
mamoliktli	elbow	**mewa**	To weed out plants (Nitla); To take out a weed (Nik) (Class 2)
mana	To place a pot on the fire; To place dishes on a table or floor (Nik) (Class 2)	**mewa**	To get up (Ni) (Class 2)
manawia	To defend (Nik) (Class 3)	**mewkatsan**	even though
manextia	To show s.t. with your hand (Nik) (Class 3)	**Mexko**	Mexico City
mapachin	raccoon	**miak**	many
masatl	deer	**miakin**	many
masesek	cold hands	**miakiya**	For something to multiple, increase (Class 2)
masewalli	native person; human	**michin**	fish
maske	even though	**michitskia**	to catch fish (ni) (Class 3)
matetik	having strong arms		

mihkwenia	To move over (Ni) (Class 3)
mihsotla	To vomit (Ni) (Class 1)
mihtotia	To dance (Ni) (Class 3)
mihxamia	To wash your face (Ni) (Class 3)
mihyokwi	To breathe (Ni) (Class 1)
mihyotia	To smell (either good or bad) (Ni) (Class 3)
miki	To die (Ni) (Class 2)
mikkatsin	dead person
miktia	To kill s.o. (Nik) (Class 3)
millah	at the corn field
milli	agricultural field
mimi	older brother
mina	To stab with a sharp stick, shoot an arrow into (Nik) (Class 2)
miston	cat
mitonia	To sweat (Ni) (Class 3)
mixiwi	To give birth (said of animals) (Ni) (Class 2)
mixtli	cloud
mohmostlah	everyday
mokwitlawia	to take care of someone (nik) (Class 3)
molinia	To move around (ni) (Class 3)
molli	chili sauce
moloni	For s.t. to boil (Class 2)
molonia	To boil s.t. (Nik) (Class 3)
monnantli	man's mother-in-law
montahtli	man's father-in-law
montli	son-in-law
morral	shoulder bag
moskaltia	To grow (Ni) (Class 3)
mostla	tomorrow

motla	To shoot s.o. (Nik) (Class 1)
motsolli	anus
moxixa	To poop (Ni) (Class 2)
moxixmiki	To really need to poop (Ni) (Class 2)
moyotl	mosquito
na	I, me
nahaya	I myself
nahnawa	To hug s.o. (Nik) (Class 4)
nakastlan	next to
nakastli	ear
nakatl	meat
nakayo	meat, flesh
namaka	To sell s.t. (Nik) (Class 1)
namakiltia	To sell s.t. to s.o. (Nik) (Class 3)
naman	now, today
namanok	just recently
namantsin	right now
namiki	To encounter s.o.; For something to meet, reach or be sufficient for something (as in catching something, medicine having a good effect, fire catching on, ceremony healing someone, have clothes that match someone) (Nik) (Nech) (Class 2)
namiktia	To get married (Nimo) (Class 3)
nanantli	mother
naneh	elderly lady

nankilia	To answer s.o. (Nik) (Class 3)	nextli	lime (needed to cook corn)
nawa	To carry s.t. on your arms (Nik) (Class 4)	ni	this, here
nawati	To speak in Nahuatl (Ni) (Class 1)	nikan	here
nawatia	To command s.o. (Nik) (Class 3)	niman	soon
nawi	4	nimantsin	soon
nawyopanya	3 days ago	no	also
ne	that	nochin	all
nechka	close by	nochipa	always
nechkawia	To get closer (Nimo); To get closer to s.t. (Nik) (Class 3)	nohnotsa	To call s.o. by phone (Nik); To be friendly and talkative (Nite) (Class 2)
nehnemi	To walk (Ni) (Class 2)	nokka	still
nehpaloa	To weave s.t. (Nik) (Class 3)	nopa	that
neka	over there	nopaya	there
neki	To want, love (Nik); To be necessary (Mo) (Class 2)	nopayah	there
nekwtli	honey	nopayoh	there
nekwtsin	bee	nopeka	there
nelliya	true, truly	nopeyoh	there
neltoka	To believe s.t. (Nik) (Class 1)	notsa	To call s.o.; invite s.o. (Nik) (Class 2)
neltokilia	To believe s.o. (Nik) (Class 3)	nowkiya	also
nelwayo	plant's roots	ochpana	To sweep s.t. (said of the cleaning ceremony with herbs) (Class 2)
nemahtli	right hand	ohome	two of each
nemi	To be out and about (Can imply someone making trouble, or an olderly man to still be active) (Ni) (Class 2)	ohtli	road
		okichtli	male animal
nemilia	To consider a problem (Nik) (Class 3)	oktik	fermented
nemilistli	life	oktiya	To ferment (Class 2)
nenepilli	tongue	okwilin	worm
nepa	there (far off in sight)	olinia	To move or bump s.t. (Nik); To have an earthquake (Tla) (Class 3)
nesi	To appear, or look like (Ni) (Class 2)		
newilia	To consider a problem (Nik) (Class 3)	olli	rubber
nextia	To show s.t. (Nik) (Class 3)		

ololoa	To roll s.t. up (Nik) (Class 3)
ololtik	rolled up
olotl	corncob (with no kernels left)
ome	2
omitl	bone
omiyo	bone (of a person)
ompa	two times
oni	To drink s.t. (Nik) (Class 1)
oniltia	To give someone a drink (Nik) (Class 3)
onkah	it exists, there are
ostoktik	having a deep hole
ostoktli	cave
ostotl	fox
otomitl	person of Otomi heritage; also slang for rude, lazy person
owaatl	sugarcane juice
owih	difficult
owihti	To have difficulty (Ni) (Class 1)
pachoa	To cover s.t.; to squash s.t. (Nik) (Class 3)
pahoni	To take medicine (Ni) (Class 1)
pahtia	To heal s.o. (nik) (Class 3)
pahtli	medicine, poison, pesticides
paka	To wash s.t. (nik) (Class 1)
paki	To be happy (Ni) (Class 2)
pakilistli	happiness
pakiltia	To make s.o. laugh (nik) (Class 3)
paktia	For something to cause you happiness (Nech) (Class 3)
palach	male turkey
palewia	To help s.o. (Nik) (Class 3)
pamitl	line

pampa	because
pan	on
panalli	bee or wasp hive
pano	To pass (Ni); To pass s.o. (Nik) (Class 1)
panoltia	To help someone pass (Nik) (Class 3)
pantia	To find s.t. unexpectedly (Nik) (Class 3)
pantsin	bread
papalotl	butterfly
pasoltik	scattered, messy
pati	something's price
patiyoh	expensive
patla	To change s.t. (Nik) (Class 1)
patlachtik	flat
patlani	To fly (Class 2)
patox	duck
patsmiki	To be sweaty, hot (Ni) (Class 2)
paxaloa	To visit s.o. (Nik) (Class 3)
payoh	bandana
pechia	To squash s.o. or s.t. (Nik); To copulate with s.o. (Nik) (Class 3)
pechpechin	frog
pehpena	To choose, pick up s.t. (nik) (Class 2)
pemoles	type of cookie
pepestik	naked
pestetl	diaper; rag
petlani	To shine (Class 2)
petlatl	sleeping mat
pewa	To begin (Class 2)

piki	To cover s.t. with a cloth, cover body with clothes or blanket (Nik); cover oneself (Nimo) (Class 2)	**posteki**	For something to break or splinter (Class 2)
		potewi	For s.t. to stink (Class 2)
pikis	bean stuffed tamal	**powa**	To read s.t. (Nik); To count s.t. (Nik) (Class 2)
pinawa	To be ashamed (Ni) (Class 1)	**powalli**	something's count, season
pinawtia	To make s.o. feel embarrased (Nik) (Class 3)	**powilia**	To recount a story, tell s.t. to s.o. (Nik) (Class 3)
pipi	older sister	**poyek**	salty
pipilolli	earring	**saka**	To transport things (Nik) (Class 1)
pipitsoa	To lick (Nik) (Class 3)	**sampa**	again
pisiltsin	tiny	**san**	just
pitsa	To blow into a wind instrument (Nik) (Class 2)	**sanilli**	story, tale, riddle, joke
		saniloa	To speak (Ni) (Class 3)
pitsaktik	narrow	**sankwalli**	just right
pitsaktsin	thing	**sankwaltsin**	normal
pitsotl	pig	**sanniman**	right after
piwia	To add s.t. (Nik) (Class 3)	**sanok**	just now
piwilia	To add to s.t. (Nik) (Class 3)	**sansehko**	together
pixka	To harvest (Ni); To harvest something (Nik) (Class 1)	**santekitl**	in any way
piya	To have s.t. (Nik) (Class 2)	**santlenweli**	whatever thing
piyali	hello, bye	**santonilli**	the next day
piyo	chicken	**sanyainon**	that's all
pohpowa	To wipe s.t. with a cloth (nik) (Class 2)	**sawa**	To fast (Ni); For leaves to fall from trees (Class 1)
poktli	smoke	**se**	one
pokyo	smokey		
polatoh	plate	**sehkanok**	apart
poliwi	To be lacking, missing, lost, or die (Ni) (Class 2)	**sehkantsin**	close by
poloa	To lack s.t. (Nech) (Class 3)	**sehsen**	each one
poloko	donkey	**sekin**	some
popochwia	To apply incense to s.o. (Nik) (Class 3)	**selia**	To receive s.t. (Nik) (Class 3)
popoka	Something produces smoke (Class 1)		

selik	unripe
semeh	I'd rather...
semilwitl	all day
semmoyawa	To scatter things (Nik) (Class 2)
semmoyawi	For things to scatter (Class 2)
sempatsin	one time
sempowalli	20
senkah	same, similar
sentel	always
sentsontli	400
senyowal	all night
sesek	cold
sesekatl	cold water
sesekwi	To be cold (Ni) (Class 2)
seseya	To become cold (Class 2)
setl	ice
setsin	one
sewi	To become cold; turn off (Class 2)
sewia	To cool s.t. off (Nik); Turn s.t. off (Nik); To sit down (Nimo) (Class 3)
seyok	another one; next
silchilli	type of small chili
siloa	to dice s.t. (Nik); to tear something up (Nik); for seeds to fall from a dry plant (Tla) (Class 3)
sintli	dry corn
siawkawa	To rest (nimo) (Class 2)
siowi	To feel tired (Ni) (Class 2)
siowilia	To get s.o. tired (Nik) (Class 3)
siowiltia	To make someone tired (nik) (Class 3)
siowiltilia	To make someone tired with work (nik) (Class 3)
sisinaltia	To piss someone off (nik) (Class 3)
sisinia	To be angry (Nimo) (Class 3)

sitlalin	star
siwapil	girl
siwatl	woman
sokitl	mud
sokiyo	dirty
sokiyoh	dirty
sosoliwi	To wear out (objects) (Class 2)
sosoltik	old, worn out object
ta	you
tahaya	you yourself
tapasolli	nest
tapasoltik	messy
tatahtli	father
tateh	elderly man
tech	right up against s.t.
teipan	later
teiskitik	hardened
teixmatkaw	relative
teka	To pay down s.o.; To pour liquid (nik) (Class 3)
tekaitta	To make fun of s.o. (Nik) (Class 1)
tekaktli	shoe
teki	To cut s.t. (Nik) (Class 2)
tekichiwa	To do work (Ni) (Class 2)
tekilia	to serve liquid to s.o. (Nik) (Class 3)
tekimaka	To give s.o. work (Nik) (Class 1)
tekipachoa	To give work to s.t. (Nik) (Class 3)
tekipano	To do work (Ni) (Class 1)
tekiti	To do work (Ni) (Class 2)
tekitl	work
tekiwah	head of village
tekiwia	To use s.t. (Nik); To be busy (Nimo) (Class 3)

tekixpoh	fellow worker; friend	tennamiki	To kiss (Nik) (Class 2)
tekohtli	boss; owner	tentsontli	beard
tekolotik	yellowish, fur-colored	tenxima	To shave or sharpen s.t. (Nik); To shave oneself (Nimo) (Class 2)
tekolotl	owl		
tekpana	To organize, stack things or people (Nik) (Class 2)	tenxipal	lips
tekpanoa	To stack, pile, organize s.t. (Nik) (Class 3)	tepalkalli	clay shards
tekpimitl	flea	tepamitl	wall
tekpin	flea	tepetl	hill
teksistli	egg	tepewi	For small things to spill out (Class 2)
tekwani	wild animal	tepexitl	canyon, cliff
tekwesoh	something sad	tepol	vulgar word, refers to male's private parts
teleksa	To kick s.o. (Class 1)	tepostli	metal
telpokatik	looking like a teenage boy	tepostototl	airplane
telpokatl	teenage boy	tepotstoka	To follow s.o. closely (Nik) (Class 1)
tema	To pour s.t. into a container (Nik) (Class 2)	teskatik	clear
temahmawtih	dangerous	teskatl	mirror
temi	To fill up; To swell (Class 1)	tetahtsin	older man
temiki	To dream (Ni); To dream s.t. (Nik) (Class 2)	tetik	strong
temiktli	dream	tetl	rock
temo	To come down (Ni) (Class 1)	tetsawia	For s.t. to tell an omen (Nik) (Class 3)
temoa	To look for s.o. (Nik) (Class 3)	tewia	To hit s.o. (Nik); To fight with (Timo) (Class 3)
temowia	To lower s.t. (Nik) (Class 3)	textli	male's brother-in-law
tenamastli	sacred three stone structure used to cook on	teyoh	rocky
tenantsin	older woman	tilana	To pull s.t. (Nik) (Class 2)
tenextik	gray	tilawak	thick
tenkawalli	leftovers	tiochiwa	To bless s.t. (Nik) (Class 2)
tenkixtia	To tell the truth (Nik) (Class 3)	tiokonew	godchild
		tionan	godmother

tiopan	church
tiotah	godfather
tiotlak	1-5 pm
tiotlakka	2-6 pm
tisi	to grind food (Nik); To grind food in general (Ni) (Class 3)
titlani	To send s.t. (Nik) (Class 2)
titlanilia	To send s.t. to s.o. (Nik) (Class 3)
tixtli	dough
tlache	what
tlachilia	To watch s.t. (Nik) (Class 3)
tlachiya	To observe, watch (Ni) (Class 2)
tlachpana	To sweep (Ni) (Class 2)
tlaeheka	To be windy (Class 1)
tlaeli	For plants to be growing well (Class 2)
tlahko	half
tlahkotona	middle of the day
tlahtlania	To ask for s.t. (Nik) (Class 3)
tlahtoa	To talk (Ni) (Class 3)
tlahtolli	word, language
tlaihyowia	To suffer (Ni) (Class 3)
tlaixpan	altar
tlaixpiya	To go to a dance (Ni) (Class 2)
tlakaki	To obey (Ni) (Class 2)
tlakati	To be born (Ni) (Class 2)
tlakatl	man
tlakayo	body
tlakemitl	blanket
tlakentia	To dress s.o. (Nik) (Class 3)
tlaki	For a plant to give fruit (Class 2)
tlakka	fruit (of a tree)
tlakwa	To eat (Ni) (Class 4)
tlakwachin	opossum
tlakwalli	food
tlalchi	on the ground
tlalia	To place s.t. (Nik) (Class 3)
tlalli	land
tlalwilia	To apply s.t. to s.o. (Nik) (Class 3)
tlamachiwa	To measure s.t. (Nik) (Class 2)
tlamachtia	To teach (Ni) (Class 3)
tlamaka	To feed s.o. (Nik) (Class 1)
tlamantli	something
tlamattsin	softly
tlamawisoa	To watch entertainment (Ni) (Class 3)
tlami	To finish (Ni) (Class 2)
tlamia	To finish s.t. (Nik) (Class 3)
tlan	if
tlanesi	For sunrise to emerge (Class 2)
tlanewi	To borrow s.t. (Nimo); To hire s.o. (Nik) (Class 2)
tlanewilia	To borrow s.t. from s.o. (Nik) (Class 3)
tlanewtia	To loan s.t. to s.o. (Nik) (Class 3)
tlani	To win (Ni) (Class 2)
tlankoch	tooth
tlankwa	To bite yourself (Nimo); To bite s.t. (Nik)
tlankwaitl	knee
tlanokiya	To have diarrea (Ni) (Class 2)
tlaoyalli	shucked corn
tlapani	For something to break in half (Class 2)
tlapasolli	nest

tlapechtli	bamboo bed	**tlaxxima**	To feel jealousy (Nimo) (Class 2)
tlapiyalli	domesticated animal	**tlayi**	uncle, sir
tlapoa	To open s.t. (Nik) (Class 3)	**tlayitl**	uncle
tlaseseya	cold	**tlayowa**	at night
tlaskamati	thank you	**tleche**	what
tlasohtli	someone spoiled in love	**tlechketl**	what
tlasolli	trash	**tlehko**	To rise, go up (Ni) (Class 1)
tlastla	To be possessive of something you love (Nik) (Class 1)	**tleika**	why
tlateillia	To tell on s.o. (Nik) (Class 3)	**tlen**	what
tlateki	To be sharp (literally, it cuts things)	**tlenweli**	whatever thing
tlatia	To hide s.t. (Nik) (Class 3)	**tlepanitta**	To respect, be proud of s.o. (Nik) (Class 1)
tlatia	To turn s.t. on; burn s.t. (nik) (Class 3)	**tliko**	on the fire
tlatla	For s.t. to burn (Class 1)	**tlikolli**	pen, ink, pencil, charcoal
tlatlasi	To cough (Ni) (Class 2)	**tlikwi**	For fire to start; machine to turn on (Class 1)
tlatoktli	something planted	**tlilli**	charcoal
tlatoktsin	moment, while		
tlatomoni	To thunder (Class 2)	**tlimekatl**	Shooting star
tlatsiwi	To be lazy (Ni) (Class 2)	**tlitl**	fire
tlatskati	To feel lazy (Ni) (Class 1)	**tlixiwitl**	comet
tlatskia	To stick (Class 3)	**tohtolon**	meatball soup
tlawaki	For a place to dry up (Class 2)	**tohwantin**	Us, We
tlawel	very	**toka**	To plant s.t. (Nik); To plant in general (Ni) (Class 1 or Class 2)
tlawelilok	trickster evil spirit	**toka**	To copulate with each other (Timo); To copulate with someone (Nik) (Class 1)
tlawelmati	To be presumptuous, overly proud (Nimo) (Class 2)		
tlawika	To owe (Ni) (Class 1)	**tokaitl**	name
tlawilli	light	**tokatl**	spider
tlaxkalli	tortilla	**tokomahtli**	squirrel
tlaxke	if not		
tlaxtlawa	To pay (Ni) (Class 2)	**tolina**	To have cravings (Ni) (Class 2)
tlaxtlen	if not	**toloa**	To swallow s.t. (Nik) (Class 3)

tolontik	round	tsakwilia	To block s.o. (Nik) (Class 3)
tomawak	fat	tsalan	under; in between
tomin	money	tsalantik	clear
tona	To be sunny (Class 1)	tsayana	To tear s.t. (nik) (Class 2)
tonalli	spirit; white hairs; show	tsayani	For s.t. to tear (Class 2)
tonanan	grandmother	tsiktik	blue
tonantsin	Virgin of Guadalupe	tsiktli	gum
tonatiw	sun, day	tsikwini	To jump up and down (Ni) (Class 2)
tonayan	during the day	tsilinia	To ring a bell (Nik) (Class 3)
topewa	To push s.t. with your body (Nik) (Class 2)	tsilintik	old but strong
topilli	staff, represents authority	tsintenno	butt
topitsin	lizard	tsipitl	bellybutton
toponi	To explode (Class 2)	tsitsimitl	person who is always angry
toroh	bull	tsokonia	To kiss s.o. (Nik) (Class 3)
tosan	gopher	tsonkalli	hair
toskak	throat	tsonkiska	someone's last name
totahtsin	priest	tsopelatl	sugary drink, juice
totatah	grandfather	tsopelik	sweet
totewkko	God	tsopinia	To inject s.o. (Nik) (Class 3)
totiotsin	deity	tsotso	bat
totolin	turkey	tsotsokatl	selfish
totomoka	To make an exploding sound (said of engines) (Class 1)	tsoyonia	To fry s.t. (Nik) (Class 3)
totomotsa	To start an engine (Nik) (Class 2)	wahka	far away
totonia	To heat s.t. (Nik) (Class 3)	wahkapan	up high
totonik	hot	wahkapanka	something's height
totoniya	To have a fever (Ni) (Class 2)	wahkapanyo	something's height
tototl	bird	wahkawa	To take a long time (Ni) (Class 2)
toyawa	To spill a liquid (nik) (Class 2)	wahkawpatl	ancestor
toyawi	For liquid to spill out (Class 2)	wahkawya	a long time ago
tsahtsi	To cry (Ni) (Class 1)		
tsakwa	To close s.t.; To place an enclosure over s.t. (Nik) (Class 2)		

wakax	cow, bull	wexka	something's size
waki	To dry up (Class 2)	weyi	big
wakka	thus	weyimati	To be conceited, egoistic, pompous (Nimo) (Class 2)
waksan	right then and there in time		
walla	To come (Ni) (Niwalki or Niwallahki)	wihtsomi	To bow your head (Ni) (Class 2)
wallika	To bring s.t. (Nik) (Class 1)	wihwitstik	prickly
wampohtli	friend	wika	To sing (Ni) (Class 1)
wan	and	wika	To take s.t. (Nik) (Class 1)
wankinon	then (after)	wikalli	the same, equal, spouse
wanya	with (in company with)	wilana	To fight with s.o. (Timo) (Class 2)
wapalli	board of wood		
watani	To snore (Ni) (Class 2)	wilotl	(1) pigeon (2) someone's penis
watsa	To dry s.t. (Nik) (Class 2)	winoh	wine or hard liquor
wawana	To scratch (Nik) (Class 2)	wiptla	the day after tomorrow
wehpolli	sister-in-law of a man, brother-in-law of a woman	wiptlaya	the day before yesterday
weli	To be able to (Ni) (Class 2)	witeki	To hit s.t. with a stick (Nik) (Class 2)
welis	perhaps	witoni	To jump (Ni) (Class 2)
welitta	To approve of (Nik) (Class 1)	wiwi	dumb
weltah	time (next time, one time, five times etc.)	wiwiitta	To treat s.o. like a fool (Nik) (Class 1)
weltiw	sister	wiyonia	To hang s.t. (Nik) (Class 3)
wentilia	To cleanse someone in a ceremony (nik) (Class 3)	xahkalli	hut
westli	woman's sister-in-law	xalli	sand
wetsi	To fall (Ni) (Class 2)	xaloh	clay cup
wetska	To laugh (Ni) (Class 1)		
wetskilia	To laugh at s.o. (Nik) (Class 3)	xamitl	corn tamal
wewentsin	old man	xantolon	Day of the Day (Sanctorum)
weweyak	long	xapoh	soap
weweyaka	something's length	xehxeloa	To divide s.t. (Nik) (Class 3)
weweyakayo	something's length	xeloa	To divide s.t. (Nik) (Class 3)
weweyaktik	long		

xikoa	To put up with (Nik); To be envious (Nimo) (Class 3)	**ya**	he, she, it, him, her
xiktli	umbilical cord	**yahaya**	he himself, she herself
xillantli	vagina	**yahmaxtik**	whole
xilotl	small green corn	**yakaatemo**	To have a cold, runny nose (Ni) (Class 1)
xilwia	To comb s.o. (Nik) (Class 3)	**yakatsolli**	nose
xima	To peel fruit, cut s.o.'s hair (Nik) (Class 2)	**yalwaya**	yesterday
xinachtli	seed	**yamanik**	soft
xinolah	non-native woman	**yane**	that very thing
xipewa	To skin an animal, skin a human, peel fruit, shuck corn (nik) (Class 2)	**yani**	this very thing
		yankwik	new
xitlaktik	straight	**yanopa**	that very thing
xitlawa	To straighten something (Nik) (Class 1)	**yawalli**	night
xitlawak	straight	**yawaltik**	round
xiwipahtli	herbal medicine	**yawatl**	night
xiwitl	plant, herb		
xiwitl	year; herb	**yayawik**	black
xiwiyo	something's leaves	**yehyekoa**	To try, taste, or practice s.t. (Nik) (Class 3)
xixa	To poop on s.t. (Nik); To poop on oneself (Nimo)	**yehyektsin**	pretty, beautiful
xochitik	flowery	**yeka**	that's why
xochitl	flower	**yekana**	To lead (Ni) (Class 2)
xochiyo	plant's flower	**yektia**	To make s.t. pure (Nik) (Class 3)
xokihyak	having a certain bad smell, similar to rotten eggs	**yewawkaw**	some time ago
xokok	sour	**yexnantli**	woman's mother-in-law
xolewa	To break s.t. apart (Nik) (Class 2)	**yextahtli**	woman's father-in-law
xolohtik	nude person	**yeyohtli**	daughter-in-law
xoloni	To get wet (Ni) (Class 2)	**yolahsi**	To reach your filling of a type of food (Nech) (Class 1)
xolotik	nude person		
xopanatl	heavy rain	**yoli**	To be alive (Ni) (Class 2)
xotla	To squash with a foot or car (Nik) (Class 1)	**yolik**	slow; slowly
xoxoktik	dark green	**yolkwesiwi**	To feel sad (Ni) (Class 2)
xoxowik	green	**yollotl**	heart

yolmelawa	To inform s.o.; tell the truth to s.o. (Nik) (Class 2)
yolpaki	To be happy (Ni) (Class 2)
yoltetik	brave, strong hearted
yoltia	To bring s.t. back to life (Nik) (Class 3)
yoltsin	boyfriend, girlfriend
yon	nor, not even
yontlen	nothing
yowalkisa	To go out at night (Ni) (Class 2)
yowalli	night
yowatl	night
yoyomitl	clothes

Vocabulary List

Resources

In recent years, a wealth of resources have sprung online, such that it would be impossible to name them all. Nonetheless, below is a list of resources that may prove to be useful for the reader.

CanalNahuatl, Tlahtoltapazolli.com

- YouTube channel managed by the author. Content in Spanish and Nahuatl with some English subtitles.

Nahuatlstudies.blogspot.com

- Blog run by Nahuatl linguist/ researcher Magnus Hansen Pharao.

IDIEZ (Instituto de Docencia e Investigación Etnológica de Zacatecas)

- Organization dedicated to research and teaching the Huasteca Nahuatl language. Courses typically offered a few times a year.

Tonelhuayo, Yolitia, Toyolxayak

- Nahuatl language magazines. Can be found online.

Nauatlachamanaltianij (KANA)

- Organization dedicated to research and teaching the Huasteca Nahuatl language. Courses typically offered once a year.

Bible.is

- Read, hear, listen to Nahuatl in various varieties. Content is christian based.

Se Ome Tlahtolli

- Nahuatl group dedicated to conducting interviews in Nahuatl, features poets, writers, lawyes, radio hosts.

RadioMás

Ecos Indígenas

- Radio Programs in Nahuatl

Trío Eyixochitl
Trío Dulce la Huasteca
Daniel Castro
Delia Ramirez Castellanos
Abdiel Valle Lara
Delia Ramírez Castellanos

- Nahuatl Musicians

Summer Institute of Linguistics (provides many resources for endangered languages)

A myriad of YouTube channels, Facebook groups, and other social media outlets.

Nahuatl Poems, Writings, Plays by:

Natalio Hernandez Hernandez
- Amo ninequi nimiquis
- Toselti ma tinemican
- Axtosel tinemi
- Nisentlachixtos

Juan Hernandez Ramirez
- Miauaxochitl
- Sempoalxochitl

Ildefonso Maya
- Ixtlamatinij
- Tlatsikuini
- Ostotl

Martin Tonalmeyotl
- Nonauatlajtol
- Kuak nikneke ninokuikatis
- Mekapapalotl
- Tlalkatsajtsilistle

Yolanda Matías García
- Xochitlajtol ika moyojlo
- Tonalxochimej

Victoriano de la Cruz
- Pedro Páramo

Eduardo de la Cruz
- Cenyahtoc Cintli Tonacayoh

Dictionaries

Oregon Nahuatl Dictionary (Wired Humanities Online Nahuatl Dictionary)
- Reliable Nahuatl dictionary, consists of Classical and Huasteca Nahuatl entries. Examples, conjugations and some audio included.

Monolingual Nahuatl Dictionary: Tlahtolxitlauhcayotl
- First monolingual Nahuatl dictionary, produced by IDIEZ.

Gran Diccionario Nahuatl
- Spanish-Nahuatl dictionary run by the UNAM University in Mexico. Focuses on Classical Nahuatl. Large database but can be difficult to maneuver.

Aulex
- Dictionary to avoid. Allows fake entries to be entered with no regulation.

Nahuatl-English Concise Dictionary
- One of the best selling dictionaries. Focuses on Classical. However, entries are not not always clear between Classical and Modern varieties.

Kwalli ohtli! - Good luck!
Kwalli xiyaw! - Go well!

Made in United States
North Haven, CT
25 February 2024

49127460R00135